Teaching Poetry in the Primary School

CA

Teaching Poetry in the Primary School

Perspectives for a New Generation

Dennis Carter

David Fulton Publishers
London

David Fulton Publishers Ltd
Ormond House, 26/27 Boswell Street, London WC1N 3JD

First published in Great Britain by
David Fulton Publishers 1998

Note: the right of Dennis Carter to be identified as the author of this work has been asserted by him in accordance with the Copyright, Designs and Patents Act 1988

Copyright © Dennis Carter 1998

British Library Cataloguing in Publication Data

A catalogue record for this book is available from the British Library

ISBN 1-85346-567-4

Typeset by Textype Typesetters, Cambridge
Printed in Great Britain by The Cromwell Press Ltd, Trowbridge, Wilts.

Contents

Acknowledgments

Firstly, acknowledgments are due to the children who, over more than thirty years, have helped me to shape my present ideas about the teaching of poetry in the primary school, particularly those in Tarvin County Primary School, Cheshire (1969–1973); Redhills Combined School, Exeter, Devon (1973–1975); and Taliesin Junior School, Clwyd (1976–1988). I have deep and powerful memories of the children and of the locations of their schools, where I enjoyed so many extraordinary moments as a teacher.

Thanks are also due to the children and teachers involved in the pilot projects of Clwyd Poetry Project (1993–1995) from the following schools: *Clwyd* – Ysgol Dunawd, Bangor-on-Dee; Border Brook CP School, Bronington VP School, Eyton VP School, Hanmer VP School, Isycoed VP School, Madras CP School, Penley; Gwersyllt CP School, Gwernaffield CP School, Mynydd Isa Junior School, St. David's RC Primary School, Mold; St. Mary's RC Primary School, Flint; Dee Road Infant School, Connah's Quay; Ewloe Green CP School, Wood Memorial CP School, Saltney; Ysgol Estyn, Hope; Taliesin Junior School, Shotton; Gwynedd CP School, Flint; Ysgol-y-Ddol, Rhydymwyn; Ysgol Croes Atti, Flint; Ysgol Glanrafon, Mold; Ysgol Gwenffrwd, Holywell and Northop Hall CP School. *Cheshire* – Huntington CP School, Chester. *Gwynedd* – Ysgol Cadnant, Ysgol Gyffin and Ysgol Bodlondeb, Conwy. To this list should be added Grafton CP School, Shropshire, where I have worked on dissemination projects since the Clwyd Poetry Project's research and development phase was completed.

Acknowledgements are also due to the sponsors of Clwyd Poetry Project, particularly The Calouste Gulbenkian Foundation, the Foundation for Sport and the Arts, Wales Arts Council, North West Arts Board and Delyn Borough Council.

I am very grateful to my co-workers on Clwyd Poetry Project, particularly the poets Rose Flint and Esyllt Maelor, the visual artist Ian Douglas, the dancer Louise Katerega, the musician Alison Wright and the drama teacher Pam Courtenay; and to Gruffydd Roberts, who co-ordinated the Project's work in the Welsh language.

Finally, I would like to thank my wife, Catherine, for her inspiring support throughout my work, particularly in her role as teacher in Gwersyllt CP, Huntington CP and Grafton CP schools.

Permission to include published poems and extracts is acknowledged to the following:
'Wild Iron' by Allen Curnow, published by Carcanet Press Limited in *Early Days Yet – Collected Poems*; 'in Just–' is reprinted from *Complete Poems 1904–1962*, by E.E. Cummings, edited by George J. Firmage, by permission of W.W.Norton & Company, copyright © 1991 by the Trustees for the E.E. Cummings Trust and George James Firmage; 'The Sea' by James Reeves is reproduced by permission of John Johnson (Authors' Agent) Limited, for the author; 'Until I Saw the Sea' from *I Feel the Same Way* by Lilian Moore, copyright © 1967 Lilian Moore, © renewed 1995 Lilian Moore Reavin,

reprinted by permission of Marian Reiner for the author; sixteen lines from 'The Ugly Child' from *The Secret Brother* by Elizabeth Jennings, published by Carcanet Press and sixteen lines from 'Dream Poem' from *Collected Poems* by Charles Causley, published by Macmillan are reprinted by permission of David Higham Associates Limited; lines from 'the african pot' by Fhazel Johennese from Voices *from Within* are reprinted by permission of Jonathan Ball Publishers (Pty) Ltd; 'Autumn Shone Forth' by Alesksay Vorobyovin is reproduced by permission of Forest Books; 'Hide and Seek' by Walter de la Mare from *The Complete Poems of Walter de la Mare* is reproduced by permission of The Literary Trustees of Walter de la Mare, and the Society of Authors as their representative; 'Overheard on a Saltmarsh' by Harold Monro is reproduced by permission of Mrs F. McGregor; 'Ducks' Ditty' from *The Wind in the Willows* by Kenneth Grahame, copyright © The University Chest, Oxford, is reproduced by permission of Curtis Brown, London; 'The Door' by Miroslav Holub is reproduced by permission of Penguin Books Ltd.

'Who alive can say,
"Thou art no poet – mayst not tell thy dreams"?
Since every man whose soul is not a clod
Hath visions, and would speak, if he had loved
And been well nurtured in his mother tongue.

John Keats, 'The Fall of Hyperion', Canto 1

Chapter One

Children and Poetry

'When we are children, people show us so many things that we lose the profound sense of seeing. Seeing and showing are phenomenologically in violent antithesis. And just how could adults show us the world they have lost! They know; they think they know; they say they know . . . . . They demonstrate to the child that the earth is round, that it revolves around the sun. And the poor dreaming child has to listen to all that! What a release for your reverie when you leave the classroom to go back up the side hill, your side hill! What a cosmic being the dreaming child is!' (Gaston Bachelard, *The Poetics of Reverie*)[1]

Poetry and the National Curriculum

This book has grown out of the work of the Clwyd Poetry Project and, in particular, its dissemination book, *The Power to Overwhelm*[2] which was published in April 1997. In it I attempt to reconcile what some observers would call the irreconcilable. On the one hand there are the demands made by poetry, the spirit of creativity and the nature and needs of children. On the other there are those made by the Education Reform Act of 1988 with its National Curriculum and, more recently, by the National Literacy Strategy (NLS) with its 'Literacy Hour'. Unless these contrary forces *are* reconciled, however, the future of poetry in schools and, more importantly, the future development of children's sensibilities are grim indeed. In order to make such a reconciliation here in this book, those two forces need to be examined.

The story begins in late 1992, by which time the National Curriculum for English was in operation but had not yet been reviewed by Sir Ron Dearing. I launched the Clwyd Poetry Project at that time as a research and development project in the teaching of poetry in primary schools. It aimed to review current practice and to broaden approaches, and it started from the hypothesis that the demands of the more formal aspects of National Curriculum English were driving teachers to neglect the subject's aesthetic elements.

The 1995 (Dearing) version of the National Curriculum for English refers to poetry here and there, but fails to consider its potential contribution to the development of pupils' language, sensibilities and dream-power. So, no rationale for the place and value of poetry in children's education appears in it. Indeed, an examination of the Level Descriptions shows that poetry was not in the minds of those who composed them. The descriptions for 'Writing', for instance, always refer to prose, as here at Level 4: 'Pupils are beginning to use grammatically complex sentences, extending meaning.'[3]

The reference here is to pupils' handling of syntax, which is the stuff of prose. Poetry, however, is written – and extends meaning to its audience – in more than grammatically complex structures. But the Level Description here makes no reference to pupils' use of imagery, rhythm, rhyme, personification, alliteration or any other poetic device. It goes on to indicate how pupils ought to spell, punctuate and do their handwriting.

To neglect poetry in this way, within the legally-binding manual for primary teachers' work in English, is to assign it minor status. Poetry is treated there as a fringe activity, one that is unlikely to figure in the 'main findings' or the 'key issues' of an Ofsted report. It was, therefore, one main aim of the work of the Clwyd Poetry Project to claim a major status for poetry in the primary school.

The minds of young children

The mind of a young child is a medium with infinite possibilities. It possesses its unique properties, drawn from its birthrights and experiences. These are beginning to make shapes. It is a mind that is acutely tuned, and it uses words acutely – as when a three-year-old draws Daddy on a pad, lifts the page, sees the imprint on the next page and calls it 'a bruise of Daddy'. What I want to emphasise by this example is the fact that a child is born with a poetic voice, which is manifest very early. It is there, for instance, in an infant's need to play with a cry or with bodily rhythms. It is there in the toddler's instinct to make a metaphorical comparison as a way of experimenting with sound and sense. When, for instance, another three-year-old calls sunlight streaming through a glass 'an angel', she is exercising her poetic voice.

The acute tuning between a young child's mind and language endures well in early life. So, by the time children come to school, their teachers' concern should not be focused exclusively on introducing them to poetry but should be equally aimed at letting loose each child's poetic voice into a poetic environment. This means not only providing poetry books and lessons but also encouraging an excited awareness of the play of language. The poetic voice exists as much in conversations as in the business of writing a poem; in the perceptions brought in from street and field as in great works of literature.

Any work of literature, whether it be written by Shakespeare or a six-year-old child, is made from a dynamic interaction between the writer (or speaker), the world and words. But the post-Dearing document and the NLS 'Framework' treat all the results of such interactions as mere language units for study. And the great weakness of such an approach to English, which seeks to describe exactly what children should be able to do at each level of their development, is that language is treated simply as a tool, and literature simply as material on which to hone it. In these two documents no aim is poetic. The whole approach is driven by programmed functions. Hence, literature is seen as having value in its fixed meanings and uses rather than in its openness to personal interpretation and response. But poetry has a far greater value than this view implies. The poetic voice in action may be more important for the future of society than most kinds of prose. This is because the poet is doing something quite different from the writer of, say, the instructions accompanying a fitted kitchen assembly kit.

When the eleven-year-old writer of the following poem, Neil, presented it to me in this 'first draft' form one morning many years ago, with pride and excitement, he was participating, at his tender age, in an ancient process by which language is replenished and renewed. Here he writes about some of the effects of the miners' strike of 1972:

'Power Cuts'
Electricity pulsates through cables,
beating in time with the turning generator.
Click! The terrible, exciting switch
that cuts out light and warmth.
Tarvin blacks out, candles light up rooms.
A candle-lit pork sausage dinner.
Grumblings as 'Dr Who' blacks out.
Washing up done in a meagre flame.
Fullup, fullup, the cards smack on the table.
'Hearts for trumps'.
Cards are played. Lost. Lost. Won.
The games go on.
The flames burn at the wick.
Wax slowly diminishes, dripping balls
of heat fall into the plate.
Feet sound on stairs, water in the basin.
Then sleep snores.

The poetic voice here re-enacts experience through the medium of language and makes of it something newly real. The value – indeed, the very existence – of such a process, as part of children's education in school, is insidiously undermined by the approaches imposed by the post-Dearing document and the NLS's 'Framework'. This book is dedicated to its defence.

Poetry in the primary school

In school, language development starts with the children's own language – the noises they make, the words they speak, the stories they tell. It is a foolish teacher who thrusts too much other language on them (even in the form of poems) too early. Children need to feel a sense of affirmation for the language and its stories that they already carry with them. Then they find it easier to absorb new language, new stories, new sounds and new worlds.

So, in seeking to develop a poetic way with language, a teacher needs to respond to the child as much as the child responds to the teacher. It is a two-way process, always. But the wise teacher will introduce plenty of poetry into the process, regularly involving the children in hearing it, reading it, writing it, speaking it and engaging with it in other ways. The essential aim is to foster each child's sense of poetry as sounds in the air as well as words on the page, and their sense of themselves as being dreamers, readers and *makers* of poetry.

Collections of books in primary schools are dominated by stories and non-fiction. The poetry section is often small, with a few books of comic verse well-thumbed. Ideally, there should be greater provision, so that a child would be almost as likely to encounter a book of poems as a book of stories or information. The same can be said of displays in school. In the plethora of signs, sayings, instructions and pupils' work, poetry is often absent. It deserves a more significant position in the visual life of schools, a number of locations where children can reflect on a piece of poetry, places for them to 'stand and stare'.

One of our major duties is, of course, the teaching of reading; and reading is more than just decoding. In a written text there is always a complex structure of awareness, attitude, know-how and sensitivity. In any poem this structure is specially important: and it is essential that we awaken children's feeling for it as we teach them to read a poem as well as how to decode, to read stories and how to use information books. Reading a poem should arouse feelings and opinions in a child and lead to the need to express and share them. So the teaching of poetry should involve the young reader in a wide variety of experiences – not only in reflective reading but also in recitation, in enactment through dance and drama, in setting lyrics to tunes, in painting imagery and in playing with ideas as well as weighing the meanings in words.

In close partnership with the teaching of reading is the teaching of writing. But, again, the highest priority here should be on equipping children with a vital means to develop their own dreamings, thoughts and feelings into active communications. Whilst being of increasing importance to the development of civilisation, writing is basically a form of expression. Everybody needs it and when children gain it they become significantly empowered members of their culture and civilisation. Without it they are reduced, and the NLS is quite right to lay so much emphasis on raising standards of achievement in writing as well as in reading.

However, there are grave dangers in an approach to teaching writing which is so obsessively focused on prose and, in particular, transactional prose. Of course, we all need to be able to negotiate the practicalities of our lives through writing as well as through talking. Yet there is a stronger demand within us to find our own characteristic voice in writing. Standardisation may oil the machinery of everyday life with its needs to earn a living and provide for our families, but without that sense of our own individual worth in the world life itself is reduced. One would only have to listen to the despairing voices of individuals calling the Samaritans to realise how profoundly important this is.

Primary schools have a unique influence in this respect, far and above any other single institution outside of the family. An individual's sense of selfness and of self value develops early and, if abused in the primary years, its recovery requires a great deal of investment. Writing, perhaps more than any other single skill, offers children in their primary schools the most powerful way of developing this sense of selfness and self value, but not if writing consists merely of answering questions and working entirely within the frame of reference provided by others.

The self-expression movement of the sixties and seventies in writing may have got the balance between the transactional and the expressive wrong in favour of the expressive, but now we are in danger of doing the same thing the other way round. Children, therefore, demand more than exercises and models provided by other people's texts. A classroom where good writing takes place *will* accommodate this but also the habitual opportunity to give voice to the dreamings from children's inner worlds and to the world which they share with each other.

For the teacher, the most important single feature in teaching reading and writing in the ways implied above is to be reflexive. In other words, teachers need to develop the habit of giving and receiving, receiving and giving, by which a reciprocal way of working is established with children. At times this may even mean relinquishing your prepared lesson because the children come to you full of something else. Daring to do that, on occasion, is a vital part of teaching poetry, which is a mutual, imaginative engagement in meaning-through-language that transcends the mere drilled study of poems written down in a book or, worse still, the filling in of cloze procedure worksheets. Unfortunately, reflexiveness is somewhat undermined by the NLS's proposals for the 'literacy hour' in which short bursts of whole class teaching are organised around longer periods of group and individual work. However, it will be in the teacher's use of her own time in that longer period where her reflexiveness will count.

The work of Clwyd Poetry Project

With such attitudes towards poetry and with these aims in mind, in late 1992 I attempted to design a more comprehensive approach to poetry in primary schools than the one promoted by current English regulations. This consists of a framework of eight modes of encounter between children and poetry as follows:

1. Listening: children listening to teachers and others reading poetry in a range of situations.
2. Speaking: speaking or singing poems or songs learnt by heart and the reading out loud from scripts.
3. Reading: poetry for teaching reading skills and for developing reading as a leisure activity.
4. Memorising: learning poetry by heart for a variety of classroom and whole-school performances.
5. Creatively conversing and conferencing: talking to learn or the exploration of meaning in poems by groups of readers, sometimes in classroom 'conferences'.
6. Expressively engaging: exploring meaning in poetry through expressive response in the artforms of dance, drama, music, visual art and writing.
7. Composing or making poems of one's own: the oral composition of poems, including young children's spontaneous poetic utterances, and composition through writing.
8. Performing/exhibiting/publishing: making work public through a wide range of performances, displays in exhibition spaces around the school and the publication of children's poetry in magazine and book form.[4]

Three surveys were carried out during 1992 and 1993: of poets working in primary schools in the United Kingdom; of the primary schools of Wales; and of the local education authorities in the United Kingdom. I believe that, taken together, these may amount to the largest survey of poetry in primary schools ever carried out. The main findings from the surveys are as follows:

- Schools and local education authorities believe that poetry deserves a higher status in primary schools. However, only a minority of schools have a policy for the use of poetry and the poets believe that the status of poetry is rather low, even though they are invited to work in schools. Teachers often leave the poets to 'get on with it'.
- Most believe that the 1988 Act had only marginal effects on the status of poetry in primary schools. Of these, half believe it was positive because of greater focus provided by INSET, and the other half believe it was 'squeezed' by the greater demands on the curriculum.
- Poets and teachers develop poetry in five ways: listening, speaking, writing, discussing and performing, but not in memorising and expressively engaging. Poetry is infrequently used in cross-curricular work and rarely linked to other arts work. It is interesting to note that the reading of poetry is not featured. Presumably, the activity of reading is 'taken for granted'.
- Poets report that children are mostly unused to writing poetry, are unfamiliar with poetic forms and mainly know only the names of contemporary comic poets. Teachers report that they introduce their pupils to a wider range of genres and poets and teach them to write it.
- Poets teach children to write using the following processes: talking; reading from their work; playing imagination and word games; acting as scribes for group composition; introducing a range of stimuli for individual writing; and stressing the importance of redrafting and of performance. The teachers use a simpler process based on class lessons on themes such as children, the seasons, the natural world, special occasions, fantasy and space. Neither the poets nor the teachers usually provide first-hand experiences. They tend to base their work on teaching simple forms such as the acrostic and on the themes.
- There was a fair amount of INSET on poetry immediately after 1988, since when it has lessened. Although many schools do invite poets to work with their children, the majority do not. Children's Book Week sometimes features a poet. Local education authority officers had difficulty in naming outstanding schools and teachers of poetry in their areas.

What should be remembered here is that these findings are based on those poets, LEAs and schools who care enough about poetry to fill in the questionnaires. In other words these findings are from the more motivated sources of opinion. The conclusions which can be drawn are mixed, but generally point to a patchy and declining role for poetry in primary schools, in which the following key elements are largely missing:

- Full engagement with a variety of poetic forms and poets of high qualit range of cultures, including our own. Comic poetry is of great value but so too are the great lyric poetry, dramatic poetry and ballads.
- A central role for poetry in the teaching of reading. For instance, why is rhyming poetry and other heavily rhythmic poetry not more widely used to develop phonic skills? Along with a more consistent provision of poetry in children's general reading diets?
- A key role for poetry within the whole curriculum. Although teachers of Key Stage 1 pupils reported using counting rhymes for teaching aspects of number, the value of poetry to make facts and experiences more memorable is overlooked.
- A wider range of modes for children to engage poetry through. Listening, speaking and writing are the main ones. A fuller engagement with poetry through, for instance, the arts would surely enrich the children's own writing as well as their all-round experience of poetry.[5]

Poetry and the National Literacy Project

So far I have presented the somewhat gloomy picture of poetry in decline in our primary schools since 1988 and offered, through the Clwyd Poetry Project's eight modes, a model for its resurgence. However, with the implementation of the National Literacy Strategy's 'Framework' in September 1998, the situation is set to change yet again. Much of this book will offer students and teachers strategies to avoid any further decline, and ways of seizing the literacy hour as an opportunity to prove that poetry has a unique and powerful role to play in developing children's literacy.

Firstly, however, we need critically to examine what the NLS is proposing to force onto primary teachers, particularly in England. NLS was established as the National Literacy Project in September 1996 by the Department for Education and Employment with the aim 'to raise standards of literacy in primary schools in line with national expectations'. Most teachers will know that this simply means the improvement of children's performances in the Standard Assessment Tasks (SATs) in English at Key Stages 1 and 2. Indeed, the introduction to the final version of the 'Framework for teaching' does not even attempt to hide the fact when it says, 'in 2002, 80% of 11-year-olds are expected to reach Level 4 or above in the Key Stage 2 English tests.'[6] The bad news for poetry here is that poetry has – so far – rarely been tested in either the reading or the writing tasks of SATs.

The three more specific aims of the NLS, which are to be achieved by the year 2002, are to raise these standards by:

i.   improving the school's management of literacy through target-setting linked to systematic planning, monitoring and evaluation by headteachers, senior staff and governors;
ii. setting clear expectations bench-marked in a term-by-term structure;
iii. improving the quality of teaching through more focused literacy instruction and effective classroom management.[7]

Judging by the draft 'Framework' produced by the NLP in October 1997, the Project team had problems with poetry, which clearly did not fit into their categories of 'Fiction' and 'Non-fiction'. This stemmed partly from a lack of clarity about poetry in the National Curriculum orders for English, in which it appears rather as a kind of fair weather visitor to primary education rather than as a fixed and reliable means of developing children's literacy. This leads to a confusion about its nature and its value. Consequently, in both the draft and final 'Framework' poetry is 'lumped together' with fiction.[8]

The largest part of the 'Framework' consists of 'The Termly Objectives', which are divided into three categories: 'Word level work', 'Sentence level work' and 'Text level work'. Apart from the use of rhyme for developing phonics and spelling in the early stages of Key Stage 1, there is no attempt to include specific poetry features in these 'Termly Objectives'. There is no 'Verse level work' and the main thrust of word, sentence and text level work is instrumental. In other words, even when poetry is included in an objective it is there largely to serve cognitive purposes rather than the poetic. For instance, take this from Year 4, Term 1 text level work: '7 compare and contrast poems on similar themes'.[6] Now this is conceived entirely as an objective exercise with little thought for the interior worlds of the poems that might be assembled around the themes. The outcome of such an objective is very likely to be one which skirts around the edges of poems without ever plumbing any depths.

However, an astute believer in poetry *can* interpret such objectives in terms of the affective needs of children and the interior worlds of the poems. So, for instance, by concentrating on the individual sound of the poems compared and the specific meanings they convey *before* making comparisons the children will develop very different attitudes and experiences of the poems. The process of making such comparisons will then be pitched at a more profound level, which will serve poetry well. The key danger here then is that poetry may be engaged narrowly by the children, and what I attempt in this book is to show teachers and student teachers how to avoid this.

Let us here also deal with that rather crude categorisation of poetry with fiction. In his letter to me earlier this year John Stannard, Director of the National Literacy Strategy, writes, '. . . . . the reason for not distinguishing poetry under a second heading is simply because we would have to write quite a number of our objectives more than once in the Framework which would make it clumsy and probably less manageable for teachers.'[9] One has to admire the honesty of Stannard here, but it does reveal a marked ignorance of the difference between poetry and fiction. It also leads to the objectives for each term's work being unwieldy and lacking in an apparent rationale either for poetry or fiction.

The lack of a rationale for poetry gives the document a piecemeal appearance as if those involved in its compilation made their decisions acting upon personal preferences and whims. Consequently, for instance, Year 4, Term 3 becomes the time when a child must learn about Japanese haiku poetry, one of the world's more subtle poetic forms. The child does so at the same time as learning about 'thin poems' – whatever they are! The great poet, Basho, was ancient by the time he mastered this most consummate of poetic forms, haiku. Here it becomes just another 'device' in a long list, including such bastard forms as the cinquain. Much poetry has been packed into the 'Framework' between draft and final versions and this is to be applauded. But much of this is ill-considered and the logic behind it contestable. Teachers must use it to their advantage rather than being intimidated by it.[6]

The very inclusion of poetry with fiction implies that they are part of the same genre and sends out many of the wrong signals about the nature of poetry. We know that poetry does tell stories, but it does so in uniquely different ways than does prose fiction. This is not to denigrate prose fiction, but to underline poetry's very different purpose. The scope of poetry is wider than that of any other kind of writing. Yes, it tells stories, but yes it also plays games with language, reflects the poet's hopes, fears, hates, loves, responses to the world and to dreams. Poetry does just about everything language can do, and even when telling stories its focus is different from that of prose fiction. For instance, when Wordsworth tells us about the leech gatherer or the old Cumberland beggar he tells us as much about his own philosophy as of the fates of those two characters. Furthermore, these are very different stories from Coleridge's 'Rime of the Ancient Mariner', which is pure fiction; and all three of these stories are told through an entirely different medium than, for instance, Jane Austen's *Northanger Abbey* or Tobias Smollett's *Humphrey Clinker* from the same period.

A similar misunderstanding informs the objectives for writing composition. The emphasis throughout these sections in the termly objectives is on the child as a sort of apprentice literary critic and imitator. There is no sense anywhere that the child has a unique vision and potential voice which is worth sharing in its own right. The balance between child as consumer of the work of others and maker of her/his own work is massively tilted towards the former. I hope to show in this book how subtle that balance must be and how it can be achieved.

So, teachers will need to be most astute in their reading and implementation of the NLS 'Framework' if they care for poetry and their children's aesthetic developments through language. However, I also wish to demonstrate that the highly concentrated focus on literacy in the NLS 'Framework' can lead to a genuine and strong engagement with poetry in our primary schools.

Perspectives offered by this book

My first perspective, which informs all I write in this book, follows up the lines from Keats's great poem 'The Fall of Hyperion' – quoted at the front of the book – with its egalitarian claim in favour of 'every man' (person) having visions to tell. Keats argues here that in order to tell these visions as a poet 'every man' needs the right kind of education in the 'mother tongue' and to be 'well nurtured' in it. I have to say that throughout my career I have believed and frequently had it confirmed that *every* child has visions worth telling. I have sought to nourish this truth and nurture every child's use of the mother tongue. This book seeks to establish a pedagogy, which I later call 'comprehensive', which is capable of achieving this fundamental aim for our children.

This is not to suggest that every child is likely to become a poet in the traditional sense, with books of his or her verse on Waterstone's bookshelves. Rather it is to claim that all children are capable of speaking and writing their visions powerfully and beautifully if we, who are charged with the duty of nurturing their use of the mother tongue, give the right kind of assistance. Many will argue that we are passing through a time when teachers are being prevented from doing so. This book tries to show how such nurturing can be achieved even at such a time.

Chapter Two of the book presents the channels through which such assistance may be provided for children. Eight such channels or modes are identified. These are introduced above but developed in much greater detail – and with examples – in Chapter Two. A particularly strong emphasis is placed on the lesser used modes of 'memorising', 'conferencing' and 'publishing' for which a broader definition is provided.

Chapter Three is about the practical steps that can be taken to open up these channels for children, from the whole business of choosing poems to share to the assessment of children's achievement. There is also a set of aims for poetry and an extensive set of eighteen learning objectives which offer a strong basis for a school's entire scheme of work for poetry from Reception through to Year 6. This is followed by suggestions for attempting the vexed question of making assessments of children's written poetry. The orders for English have no statements in the writing levels which address the writing of poetry. This book does and puts them to use with actual examples of children's poems. Chapter three concludes with practical advice for negotiating a way through the literacy hour using poetry in ways which make it intellectually challenging and exciting.

Chapter Four develops the most comprehensive range of materials for teaching poetry in the literacy hour that has yet been produced. There is highly detailed advice about preparing for and conducting a poetry literacy hour and material for a week's lessons for each year group from Reception through to Year 6. Each of these sets of materials includes suggestions for taking the work beyond the literacy hour into the arts of dance, drama, art and music.

In Chapter Five the book returns the reader to the minds, imaginations and dreaming potential of children, using the work of the French philosopher Gaston Bachelard as a touchstone. It attempts to locate the first place for the development of literacy inside the heads of children rather than outside them in some office in the DfEE or National Literacy Strategy premises in Reading. It argues in favour of reverie or 'day-dreaming' as an influential power in shaping the emerging reader and writer and, again, shows how students and teachers can put such concepts into practice even on a four-week teaching practice! It argues for the critical value of poets' works in this process and demonstrates how this can be achieved.

The theme of Chapter Six of the book is children's experience of the world about them. Referring to the poetry of Seamus Heaney in his collection *Seeing Things*, it argues that, like the other arts, poetry can transform the ordinary. The transformation of the ordinary into something amazing, it claims, is also a natural thing for children to do. Here, ways and means of focusing this tendency in children are outlined and demonstrated right down to more actual lesson outlines. The use of poets' work, again, is shown to be of vital importance in the whole process.

The book's appendices supplement all the practical detail in its main parts with lists of further poems to use and books of poetry for the classroom and library.

The publishers, David Fulton, and I have wished to create here a book which will motivate students and teachers to raise the profile of poetry in their schools, excite their children through it and make it a vital tool for developing literacy.

References

1. Bachelard, G. (1969) *The Poetics of Reverie*, Beacon Press, Boston, USA.
2. Carter, D. (1997) *The Power to Overwhelm*, Clwyd Poetry Project (CPP), Mold.
3. DfEE (1995) *English in the National Curriculum*, HMSO, London.
4. Carter, D. (1997) *The Power to Overwhelm*, Clwyd Poetry Project (CPP), Mold.
5. Carter, D. (1994) **i**. (February) *A survey of the experiences encountered by and the attitudes of poets who visit primary schools in the United Kingdom*, CPP, Mold. **ii**. (November) *A survey of the value placed on poetry in primary schools by local education authorities in the United Kingdom*, CPP, Mold. **iii**. (December) *A survey of attitudes towards and use made of poetry in the primary schools of Wales*, CPP, Mold.
6. Stannard, J. (1998ii) *The National Literacy Strategy, Framework for Teaching*, The National Literacy Project, Reading.
7. Stannard, J. (1997) *Framework for Literacy* (draft), The National Literacy Project, Reading.
8. Stannard (1997 and 1998ii). – see 7. and 6.
9. Stannard, J. (1998i), Letter of 20.1.98, National Literacy Project, Reading.

Chapter Two

Ways of Working with Poetry

The Clwyd Poetry Project surveys indicated that when poetry is taught at all in primary schools it is done so in a piecemeal fashion, that there is generally no rationale for its use. Consequently, children are often expected to write poetry without having any depth of experience to draw on. Subsequently, when they are told not to rhyme because this distorts the sense of what they are writing, they can be forgiven for being confused and producing plain prose in shorter lines. This is why so many thousands of teachers do not like developing poetry-writing with their classes. Their pupils often have no notion of what poetry is, other than the nursery rhymes and songs they learnt by heart in nurseries, playgroups and infant classrooms.

This brings me to the important consideration of how the notion of poetry may be established inside a child's head. One of the ways of working which I suggest here is that of memorising and I would like strongly to emphasise this here. In his review of Helen Vendler's book about Shakespeare's sonnets, George Steiner applauds the stress she places on readers memorising the sonnets. He writes of 'the unique values and joys of memorising the texts we love' and claims,

> What we know by heart cannot be taken from us . . . . . Learning by heart makes of us direct partners to Shakespeare's enterprise. The voices offered to us in his 'lyric script' only become thoroughly real when transposed into our own, into the active echo which memory empowers.[1]

If children are involved regularly in learning poems by heart there are significant benefits for the development of their all-round literacy. Each poem, as it were, lays a track of highly wrought literary language in their minds. Over time, the accumulation of these language tracks will affect much of the language use around it. The educational gains for children are many. They will gain possession of a growing resource of powerfully contextualised vocabulary. The mind is more ready and quick to supply the writer with words and phrases from this hoard when he or she is under the pressure to write, than it is to produce words learnt from lists with definitions. Such words and phrases are not merely units to put into place when required. They are resonant with the meanings and relationships they had in the original poems. If the original poems have been learnt in a joyous, excited way then those words and phrases are also likely to be steeped in joy and excitement. This goes a little way to explain one poet's influence over another.

Such memorised poems are also a reminder to children of the direct relationships which exist between words, meanings, the senses and emotions. Thus the written word appears as something more important, as something to look up to like the minister with his huge Holy Bible on the lectern. And tracks they *do* become, tracks which can be travelled over and over again with a real sense of partnership in such journeys, partnerships with the great visionaries of the past.

These language tracks can be used to convey children in directions of their own choosing. As Steiner says, 'memory empowers', in this case the children's own use of the written word. Such tracks become whole and specific pieces of learning which are transferable. Children need such actual pieces of learning to substantiate more generalised rules which govern much of their learning, particularly in reading and writing. Steiner calls such learning 'a proud tradition of humanistic scholarship'.[2]

Learning by heart, however, is here offered as a part of a whole approach to poetry in the education of primary children, along with the following modes of encounter:

Listening

There are many tapes of spoken poetry available, which can make a positive contribution to this aspect of a teacher's work in poetry. It is also valuable for children to hear a range of people speaking poetry. However, the greatest responsibility for children's access to good quality readings of poetry lies with the teacher. She can create in most children a lifelong love of poetry. It is, therefore, important to 'get these occasions right'. A close friend of mine recalls with animation a little old Irish nun reading from Longfellow's 'Hiawatha' at his primary school. He ascribes much of his love of poetry to her great and obvious relish for the rhythm of the poem, which she read in her soft Irish voice.

Teachers and student teachers should, therefore, practise reading poems to themselves before reading them to the children. They should strive to put feeling and animation into every reading so that the children will witness a key person in their lives demonstrating commitment to the poems. Rehearsal always enhances performance. Some of these poems should be learnt by heart as this will lead to an enhanced performance. The teacher will then be able to animate her speaking of the poem far more, through facial expression and body language. Consequently, the children will have direct contact with her and will be able to 'catch' the animation she puts into her speaking of the poems. Such experiences will go deeper into the children's memories and will have more effect on the formation of their attitudes towards poetry than almost anything else she may do. They will remember her putting passion or humour into the words. It will be a special time out of which their own commitment can germinate and grow.

Speaking

From such performances the children will also learn how to speak poetry themselves, but this set of skills should not be left to chance. A process needs to be established whereby the children listen, read, learn by heart and speak poetry regularly. This will make a vital contribution to their development in speaking, listening and reading. It will also develop them as poets in their own right because the rhythms, images and cadences which they are hearing, learning and speaking regularly will affect the way that they develop their own poetry.

A much neglected aspect of the speaking of poetry is what used to be known as 'choral speaking'. In Wales this neglect has not occurred because of the Eisteddfodau, competitive musical and poetry events which take place in all schools and in most villages and towns. Most children in Wales, therefore, have plentiful opportunities to learn and speak poetry both individually and in groups. It is noticeable, particularly in Welsh-medium schools, how well the great majority of children 'speak out' on all sorts of public and semi-public occasions, because of this tradition.

In literacy hour lessons the initial sharing of a poem should involve choral speaking, using combinations of voices ranging from solos to the whole class in unison. The children's speaking voices should be blended to make the most of the various sound combinations possible and this should be matched to the content of texts. Children also need to learn to vary and even change their voices to create particular effects. For instance, in James Reeves's 'The Sea', which is set out as a lesson for Year 2 in Chapter Four of the book, they might speak the word 'moans' in 'The giant sea-dog moans' in a whining dog voice. To create the feeling of a 'giant' dog a large number of voices would be combined. On the other hand, in the third verse of that poem the children's voices might speak almost in a whisper for 'But on quiet days in May and June' or, alternatively, the whole verse might be spoken solo, one child's voice for each line. There are many possibilities. There are strong links here with music, the speaking of poetry being akin to singing, and over time the class should become an accomplished choir of speaking voices with the children fully aware of the interpretive possibilities of their voices.

An integral part of 'conferencing' (presented separately) in the group work session of a literacy hour can be the group of children working out how to speak poems. As they become more experienced performers, the children can be asked to organise their voices so as to convey the meanings they find in the poem. They will then be dealing with the sounds of the poems and how they relate to the meanings. If they engage in this as part of their work in speaking and listening, they will become clearer and more confident readers and speakers in assemblies, concerts and services throughout the school year.

Reading

All work in poetry will require the children to read poems, and poetry can play a major role at the heart of children's reading development. Reading schemes have tended to dwell too much on prose, often to the exclusion of poetry altogether. Yet research studies in recent years have proved the value of poetry to the development of reading skills. When very young children encounter texts, they find it far easier to tackle them if they are strongly rhythmic. If they have a marked rhyming element, this makes it easier still. The rhythms and the rhymes increase the predictability of a text and predictability is a vital aspect of learning the basic skills of reading.

There has been a growing re-emphasis on the value of phonics recently, but poetry has not featured centrally in the debate even though it provides the most fertile resource for developing children's awareness of phonics. Much comic verse and many nursery rhymes provide higher quality phonic material than, for instance, the Dr Seuss books, being written out of inspiration rather than to service reading schemes. Such poems have a lasting appeal to children. In my experience children quickly tire of, say, 'Fox in socks', whereas the delights of the Quangle Wangle are with us all our lives. Furthermore, comic verse and nursery rhymes prepare children for the whole field of poetry.

There are, however, dangers in using such poems merely for their *use* in teaching reading. It is easy to use the rhyming pattern in a poem merely to service the teaching of a sound, leaving the meaning of the poem itself behind. The likelihood here is that the world of the poem will not be absorbed by the children and even the sound its rhyme reinforces may be forgotten. However, if the children work inside the poem on its content and its implications, its infrastructure of sounds and patterns will become embedded. There is a further implication, too. The teacher who only wishes to reinforce a phonic blend is very likely to choose any old poem to do it, irrespective of its quality as a work of poetry. Thus poetry and literature generally become mere instruments and their influence declines.

When children have moved on from the business of cracking the codes of reading and are independent readers they may take one of two directions. Many read stories and novels, and some read, almost exclusively, from non-fiction. Poetry books then become resources for occasional reading, or something to look at after the work is over, or to go to as a last resort. A fuller reading experience in the primary school, including poetry books at the heart of every child's reading programme, is greatly to be desired.

Memorising

Here I feel I need to re-emphasise what I claimed above and say that many of the suggestions and discussions in this book imply the need for children to learn poems 'by heart'. It is a neglected aspect of school poetry. In the 1950s and before, the learning of poetry was part of the curriculum but the context for this was often on a par with doing mental arithmetic and spelling tests. I well remember myself having to recite my verses to the teacher on a Friday morning and feeling embarrassed when I got them wrong.

However, every poetry-loving adult I know has, as it were, many islands of poetry in his or her imagination and will at times eagerly speak them aloud, often with a passion informed by nostalgia. It is a lasting pleasure to such people. But there is more to it than this. Having these poetry structures in one's mind affects the use one makes of language itself. For instance, Churchill's wartime speeches were shot through with influences from the poetry he knew by heart. It contributed to his rhetorical style and was not only present in his direct quotations. How could the famous lines, "Never in the field of human conflict has so much been owed by so many to so few" be composed by a mind not steeped in poetry learnt by heart? It was Churchill's own rhetoric, but it arose partly out of his experience of poetry.

There are many occasions in the general life of a school when the children will need to learn poems by heart. In many of their songs, hymns and prayers they already do. What I am suggesting here is that this can be greatly extended, to take in many of the genres of poetry which may be used in classroom work.

Creatively conversing and conferencing

If poetry is at the heart of English work, there will be many occasions when it is discussed. The context for this will usually be an open forum, led by the teacher, with children joining in if they have something to say and the confidence to say it. Other discussions may involve children in twos or threes talking informally about a poem they have read or written. Although natural and widespread, both methods have drawbacks. The open forum only ever affords talking opportunities to a minority of articulate, willing and self-confident children. No matter how good the teacher may be at managing these forums, there will always be a silent majority. And the informal chat about poetry often leads nowhere, particularly if the children are inexperienced. Both methods have their place but for effective conversation the class conference provides an enhanced model.

The idea of conferencing in schools arose in the 1980s as a result of the National Oracy Project's work[3], but its origins go back to the 1970s and the work of writers such as James Britton[4] and Douglas Barnes[5]. The advantages of conferencing are that it offers the possibility of small group discussion with a degree of formality and maximises the number of real participants in the talk. If used as a regular teaching technique, not only in poetry but in every area of the curriculum, all the children will benefit. They will quickly understand how to do it and that everybody is expected to speak at some, if not all, stages. Conferencing can be effectively started in Year 2 and this is how to do it:

1. Divide the class into groups of four or five children who are able to work and talk together.
2. Each group chooses a scribe who writes out the ideas and feelings of the group to report back to the class later. This job should revolve so that every child does it at some time.
3. The children read the poem silently to themselves first, with help provided to those who require it. Then they read out loud, taking turns and helping each other.
4. They pause for a moment to take it all in. Then they take themselves on a sort of mental walk through the poem. It should be like a leisure walk in which, every so often, you stop and focus on something (as one does, for instance, in a castle with its information boards).
5. They might stop to focus through discussion on the following sorts of things: a story; new ideas or new ways of expressing old ideas; images based on our senses; rhythms and rhymes and other sound structures; personal feelings evoked and responses provoked; anything else that pops into their heads, if relevant.
6. Encourage the children to explore the poem without fear of being wrong or making fools of themselves. At first you could say that each child in the group should contribute at least one thing to the discussion and that anything that is said, so long as it is seriously intentioned, is right enough.

7. When the groups have held their meetings and the scribes have noted down the main points, they join for a plenary session in which the scribes present their own group's conclusions.
8. The teacher notes the main things each group says about the poem and attempts a summary, then adds her own feelings and ideas and allows further comments. It will help if you read and consider the poem beforehand so that your ideas are clear to the children.
9. If the children wish to take this even further they might, in collaboration, write a short summary of what they have read and talked about, then provide copies for the class poetry file and their own individual files, but it is important not to make this into a regular and obligatory chore.

The benefits of such an approach are stronger when each group conferences a different poem. That way the whole class has contact with several poems rather than merely one. However, sometimes and with certain important poems it may be necessary to conference one poem.

Expressively engaging

In many of the Clwyd Poetry Project pilot studies dance, drama, visual art and music were seen to have enlightening contributions to make to the exploration of meanings in poems. This has been one of the more significant findings in the three years of the pilots. Drama, for instance, was shown to have a body of practice with which to open up to children human experiences contained in poems from cultures as diverse as the early dynasties of Ancient China and Welsh mining communities between the wars. Similarly, visual art was seen to provide ways to illuminate the complexity of Shakespeare's imagery in *Hamlet*.

Bachelard writes: 'a poetic image can be the seed of a world'.[6] To participate in such new worlds one needs to become a reader of poems, in order, in Auden's words, 'to share in the secondary worlds' of others.[7] Children, however, are inexperienced readers, even the best of them, and need assistance. That is one reason why they go to school and learn from teachers. In the past, the assistance children have sometimes received in this great development in their lives has failed to gain them entrance into these worlds. The approach based solely on the comprehension exercise and the essay of literary criticism was always more likely to reduce poems and other literature to a rubble of printed words, to be scrambled over to complete the task and get a good mark.

The arts of drama, dance, art and music offer different, more active ways of reading works, through the making of new work, which is both an act of comprehension and re-creation at the same time. For instance, a group of Year 5 and 6 pupils during Clwyd Poetry Project's 'Imaginary Worlds Project' made a dance based on Blake's 'Tyger'.[8] This involved the children in a great deal of discussion with their teacher and a visiting dancer about the meanings in the poem.

The children were struck by the vivid pictures projected by the poem of the tiger's face, of the 'forest of the night', the 'immortal eye', 'dread grasps' and the like. Their resulting dance drama consisted of one group speaking the memorised words rhythmically, while the dancing group interpreted each major image. Firstly, they made a symmetrical *tableau* of staring tigers, which became a large circle, sank and broke into smaller groups, which made moving pictures out of the images: tangling forest, immortal eye, anvil-hammering, spear-throwing, dread grasps, sinew-twistings . . . . . Such work would not have been possible without the children exploring meanings in the imagery of the poem. Each art form provides a means to explore understanding through making, and later I will show how the arts can serve their part alongside the more formal 'literacy hour' kinds of approach.

The most powerful way to respond to poems through, as it were, re-making the ideas in them, or taking those ideas further, is through writing itself. There are dangers in this, however. If children only write poems in response to the poems of others they lose the opportunity to set their own agendas. On the other hand, many children, particularly those who have little experience of writing poetry, can be intimidated by the request to write a poem. They may have no real notion of what that invitation really means, other than a vague sound or picture in their head of something which rhymes. If they then write in tortured rhyme and meet with a pained response from their teacher or a visiting writer their lack of confidence may well be compounded.

Every poet who ever wrote owes a lasting debt to his or her favourite poets. Biographies of poets are testament to this. Keats, for instance, used to prowl around his room reading Spenser, Milton or Shakespeare during those times when his inspiration had faded. Heaney in 'Feeling into Words'[9] acknowledges his happy debts to Gerard Manley Hopkins. Children also need models but this presents teachers with a dilemma. On the one hand they may be enjoying their Spike Milligan, Michael Rosen and Roger McGough – and who can blame them? But on the other hand they are never going to find their own poetic voice using such writers as models. The teacher has, perhaps, to encourage the reading of certain poems for sheer enjoyment at the same time as carefully choosing poems and extracts of poems as models when trying to develop the children's own writing. A balance has to be struck between the two and on the teacher's side there needs to be poems chosen for their quality.

Such poems – and there are many discussed here – will form the bedrock of the entire poetic enterprise and their importance can not be overstated. A simple example is provided by a group of Year 3 and 4 children in a lesson based on Allen Curnow's 'Wild Iron'.[10] Here is the poem:

> Sea go dark, go dark with wind.
> Feet go heavy, heavy with sand,
> Thoughts go wild, wild with the sound
> Of iron on the old shed swinging, clanging:
> Go dark, go heavy, go wild, go round.
> Dark with the wind, heavy with sand,
> Wild with the iron that tears at the nail,
> And the foundering shriek of the gale.

'Wild Iron' was chosen as a good example of a poem about bad weather, but the teacher devoted the first part of the lesson to the children's pure enjoyment of its features. It was chanted in various ways with various effects, the wailing scream on 'shriek' being a particular favourite. In the next part of the lesson the children talked about what they thought it was about, most of them deciding it was a storm at the coast with very high winds. The teacher told them that 'foundering' really means ships sinking, a grim realisation for the children. Key poetic features were also discussed and searched out and the children saw that its echoing rhythm was its most noticeable feature.

Some time was spent, also, looking at the nouns, adjectives and verbs in the poem and this was no mere analytical exercise for the sake of knowledge about language. It revealed, for instance, the following adjectives, each repeated several times: 'dark', 'heavy' and 'wild'. This revelation underlined the grimness of the poem's mood. It revealed that the verb 'go' is repeated eight times, thereby pointing to the voice of the poem as one urging these wild things to happen. 'Who is saying these things?' is a question with almost a demonic answer.

The children had recently experienced appalling weather themselves, but in the countryside: constant heavy rain, flooding, high winds bringing trees down, loss of electricity and falls of snow. They were invited to write a poem about their own experiences and, although the teacher didn't lay down rules, he did suggest that they try to put rhythm into their poems as 'Wild Iron' had so much rhythm in it. One child, Louise, whose work had never shown much trace of rhythm before, was mightily impressed with 'Wild Iron' and wrote:

Mud so deep, deep with rain.
Snow so soft, soft like the sky.
Ice so slippy, slippy like the road.
Deep, heavy rain.
Deep heavy mud.
I wonder what's next.
Frozen pets, pets so cold,
Chickens feathers, feathers made of ice.
Heavy wind.
Heavy snow.
Oh no!

Her work begins with a pure echo of Curnow's, but as she develops her ideas she takes possession of its rhythm too and departs from Curnow's model. Consequently, much of the poem becomes her own. She has learnt much about rhythm in poetry, but also has found a way of making her ideas and feelings have voice.

Composing or making poems of one's own

The issue of how to get children writing their own poems is a complex and controversial one and I will be returning to it a number of times throughout the book. However, here I would like to establish a few first principles.

The most vital dilemma concerns ownership or control of the act of writing. During the 1960s many teachers misinterpreted 'creative writing' and the child-centred approach, appearing to believe that it meant hardly teaching children anything at all. They thought that all a teacher had to do was to provide a stimulus and wait for the child's response. When the result was thirty versions of banality they often wondered why. But this was always a gross misunderstanding of the principles of great pioneers like Herbert Read and Christian Schiller. In many books of the period children's poems of profound insight can be found.[11] The problem was that too many teachers 'jumped on the bandwagon, who didn't know how to play any of the instruments'.[12]

The other end of the spectrum is seen in the whole-class brainstorm on the blackboard, in which the children help the teacher compose a poem. As an exercise this has limited worth if ideas are written up which are subsequently recycled by each child. Children need to assume some control over their expressive agenda and this brainstorm approach makes the teacher too powerful. In such lessons the children do not have space to exercise their imaginations because they are crowded out by the brainstormed ideas of others. This approach flourished in the 1980s, which saw a number of publications about the teaching of poetry of a practical, 'how to do it' kind. I am sure that in the right hands they led to good work in schools. Yet their emphasis was really on tips for playing particular word games and in the wrong hands made the process of children making poems no more expressive than doing sums.[13]

The most reliable sources of expertise are the poets themselves and teachers and students can do no better than base their approach to teaching children how to write poems on Ted Hughes' advice in *Poetry in the Making*. Here, he urges writers to have faith in their own imaginations and the words which they already have. He writes 'let the words look after themselves'. For Hughes the moment of the making of a poem should not be cluttered with self-consciousness or obsession with the formality of vocabulary, spelling, punctuation and grammar. He argues for a kind of engagement in which the senses are fully switched on. 'You do not look at the words,' he writes, 'You keep your eyes, your ears, your nose, your taste, your touch, your whole being on the thing you are turning into words.' In other words, your energy goes into the reverie and not into the language you are using.[14]

Letting the words look after themselves is essential for the moment of the making of the poem. But after that – and only after that – attention to the words themselves becomes important. After the first phase of composition is complete, it will be natural to apply the craft of poetry-making to it so long as the poem is worth it. But there is a right order in this matter. No poet leaves a good poem in its first form. On the other hand no poet would be scrambling around in the thesaurus in the first phase of a composition.

The approach to poetry-making advocated by Ted Hughes can be called 'improvisation' in which the writer goes into a 'headlong, concentrated improvisation on a set theme'. His method aims to develop in children the 'habit of all-out flowing exertion for a short, concentrated period, in a definite direction'.[15] Most children find this exciting once they know the rules but, when making a start, teachers may prefer to give the children the security provided by a group or whole-class approach in which each individual provides one or two ideas for a 'composite' poem. Indeed, it can be useful to start each session with a quick improvisation on a given theme in which each child finds one idea or image.

This improvisational approach is a flexible and powerful way of getting children composing, no matter what the objects of their attentions. They might be contemplating something which is entirely in their memories. Or it might be shells from the beach or characters in poems or stories. These are all 'objects' which the children are turning into words. Each requires a similar single-minded concentration and 'all-out flowing exertion'. Although the thought processes may be different, more direct in the case of shells than memories or characters from literature, the way of working is the same. What the teacher is doing is trying to enable the children to enter a state of meditation on the theme of the object, whatever it is, and to write out of that meditation.

The business of drafting and redrafting can cause problems, but some kind of reworking is often necessary, especially for any pieces which the children wish to develop into full works for an audience. The problems come when teachers expect their children to redraft everything they write and when they make it clear to the children exactly what should and what should not be kept in and developed further. The poem then begins to cease being the child's poem. The great danger is that the children will assume the teacher's taste and change their work according to that. Then they will lose ownership a little and technique will become more important than their own ideas. However, if the kind of programmes suggested in this book are put into practice, children's own awareness of what is good and what is bad will, in time, grow strong.

In addition to matters such as spelling, punctuation, bad expression and handwriting, teachers' most productive contribution to re-drafting may well be to assert a few basic principles. So, when poems are being redrafted a teacher might, for instance, urge children to avoid using words which don't really serve the purpose or ones which make the lines weak. They might teach their children about clichés and how they weaken work. However, there are no short-cuts to this. Usually it will involve getting into a dialogue with a child about the poem. Just as artists develop ideas in sketchbooks most poets write in notebooks and this is a valuable model for composition work in schools. Poetry composition is always at its best in the primary school when teachers are able to move away from the set-piece lesson around the blackboard. The aim should be to develop the autonomy of the children as poets. They should be encouraged to carry their notebooks with them at all times and to be on the 'look-out' for poems.

Even if a teacher has to work with her whole class to timetabled lessons, she can provide a diversity of objects for the children's attention as often as possible. Sometimes, of course, it is essential to work together, particularly when introducing new ideas and approaches. On such occasions teachers should continue to stress individuality of expression, that there is no right or wrong way of responding to a given object. The use of notebooks will emphasise this. Each notebook should be different, being a sort of trail of experience and expression.

Performing, exhibiting and publishing

Much has been written about 'a sense of audience' during the last fifteen years or so and the work of the National Writing Project of the 1980s placed this idea firmly in the National Curriculum English document.[16] It is closely connected to the process of redrafting, but there are dangers if the 'sense of audience' is forced on children at the compositional stage of making a poem. It is better to develop the idea of audience as part of the redrafting stage of those pieces which teachers and the children wish to develop further.

Ultimately, poets, like all writers and artists, need to 'publish' their work. Traditionally, this has been in magazine or book form, but here I would like to develop the concept of publication a little further. To publish means to make your work public, to share it with others. This is an important part of the whole process of composition. Without it writers and artists are, in a way, cut off from others in terms of their work. This applies in equal measure to children. For children publication is an important part of validation, of the sense of becoming something in the world, of the development of self-esteem.

In a contemporary school the act of publication may take any or all of three basic forms: live performance of works to audiences; exhibition in classrooms or other parts of the school; and the printing of works for circulation. However, in his book *Assessing Achievement in the Arts* Malcolm Ross identifies a fourth: children discussing their work with teachers and others.[16] This strikes me as an essential part of the process of making poems. There should be an ongoing dialogue between teacher and child. Although that dialogue may occasionally need to turn into an instructional monologue from the teacher, it should normally be one in which the teacher's ideas of rightness do not take over the child's concept. So, the teacher needs to be more reactive than proactive in this. It is a subtle part of any teacher's work, which Ross's book illustrates.

A good example of this idea of children talking about their work as another, important way of publishing it was provided to Clwyd Poetry Project in a pilot project in Conwy. The following poem, about the rain was written in Welsh by a seven-year-old English-speaking child, David:

Cysgu, cysgu	Sleeping, sleeping,
Mae'n bwrw glaw	It's raining.
Mae ysbryd y glaw	The ghost of the rain
Wedi dod yn y dydd.	Has come in the daytime.
Mae glaw fel gwn	The rain is like a gun
Sydd ddim wedi tanio,	Which has not been fired.
Mae glaw yn stompio	The rain stamps
ar yr atmosffer	on the atmosphere
Fel cawr mawr,	Like a big giant.
Mae glaw fel drwm	The rain is like a drum
mawr, mawr.	very large.
Mae can y glaw	The 'song' of the rain
yn piter pater	Is pitter-patter
Trwy y dydd.	Through the day.

Weithiau mae glaw yn mynd	Sometimes the rain goes
Tu mewn i'r pyllau dwr	Inside the puddles.
Mae pyllau dwr	The puddles
Yn dy i'r glaw.	Are a house for the rain.
Weithiau mae glaw wedi diflannu	Sometimes the rain disappears.
Mae'r glaw yn mynd	The rain goes
i fyny ac i fyny,	up and up.
Ta-ta glaw!	Goodbye rain.

After it was finished the child talked in Welsh with his teacher about this poem and his use of the language showed the same assurance as in his writing. The following, in which the teacher (T) and the child (C) reflect on the making of the poem and its meanings, shows the value of conversation both as a means of publication and a way of developing poetic insight further:

T: I'd like to talk about your poem – Rain. Why did you choose that title?

C: Because everyone was doing a project about rain. Rain is nice and I like it and I think I can make poetry about the rain to tell everyone else that rain makes everything nice.

T: Sleep – sleep – the ghost of the rain. Why ghost?

C: I've sort of made a picture out of black clouds and rain (*in his imagination*) because the black clouds are shaped like a ghost and rain gives eyes, nose and mouth to him.

T: That's interesting . . . . . What about this line – an unfired gun?

C: Well, when the rain goes inside the storm it stamps about like a gun. It stamps on the atmosphere.

T: You like that word atmosphere.

C: Well, I – um.

T: You're not sure about this word?

C: I like it when rain stamps about . . . . . I think . . . . . like on the atmosphere. (*Has problems with Welsh.*)

T: I liked the bit 'can y glaw', the song of the rain.

C: Yes, well the song of the rain, sort of like it goes 'six block', 'one block'. It's not just doing 'one plonk', 'one plonk', 'one plonk'.

T: Like a pattern? Like a piece of music?

C: It's not just coming down in one plonk. It's not straight. Not like a waterfall, not like it goes down.

T: I like that. It gives the picture straight away. Now this is interesting: 'the rain falls into the puddles. The puddles are a home to the rain.' What does this mean?

C: Well, I've given life to the rain. When people go inside a house and teachers go into the staffroom it's like a house (puddle) and I've given a house to the rain and the house is the puddle. There's a family there because there's a lot of raindrops and they're like a family.

T: Marvellous! I would never have thought of that. You have thought hard about the poem. How have you come to these ideas?

C: I just get an idea and I think, 'Oh, I must jot them down'. I don't think about fitting it in but it all comes together. After finishing writing poetry I don't really care.

T: You don't worry. You just enjoy . . . . . Why did you choose 'i fyny i fyny' (up and up)? Rain usually goes down.

C: Well, when there's sun it disappears, the rain and the puddles. I didn't want every word in the poem to be about raining and I've chosen the sun to come out and disappear the rain.

T: Shooting it away? How did you feel at the end of the poem?

C: I did not like it completely. It was sad.

The teacher reports on the child's excitement on hearing himself holding this conversation in Welsh. He says, 'I didn't realise I could speak Welsh like that'. The teacher and child went on to discuss another poem he had written. This time the conversation was in English. In that poem he writes the line 'Let go your life as a prisoner in Winter' and this is his reflection on it:

C: Yeah, well, I just got this funny feeling and vision of this big, big steel wall that nothing could get through and these bars and little window with all these bars and everybody in the world just clamp holding onto them and this great big hand holding onto them inside and it was all in winter and it came to spring and the wall just shot open and the hand just opened and they just 'let go their lives as a prisoner in winter.'

These conversations between teacher and child show him revisiting the concepts in the poem, rather than merely commenting on it. There is a sense in which the ideas and images in the poems are investigated further. Children of this age rarely keep ideas in fixed form. They either lose interest and move on or, if invited to revisit an idea, rediscover the feeling behind it and continue to develop it. The conversation, although reflecting on the poem, is a growth in its own right. It reflects, consolidates and then re-develops. The value of this to the process of arts education is that the teacher is showing a well-focused interest in the child's work. According to Malcolm Ross: 'Interest, curiosity, attentiveness and arousal are all manifestations of praise; they are formative; they build, stimulate, motivate and facilitate satisfaction'. The child was 'thrilled' by the conversation, felt validated, praised . . . . . Ross goes on to say:

Praise has always been understood as an important response to art. Here we have come to understand it interactively, as vital reciprocation, as central to the sharing that enables the pupil then to differentiate . . . . .[17]

Finally, there is the value such conversations have to the development of poetic perception. When writing the poems, the child, like a poet, works intuitively rather than objectively. But his intuitions are continually fuelled by what he experiences of the world and of poetry itself. Reflecting on his own work with a sympathetic teacher – who validates and praises it – the child adds new thought, new perception to those original intuitions. Not only that, he increases his facility to move between objective thinking and subjective feeling and between the surface of a poem and the depth of its meanings.

A productive education in poetry will involve children in reading their work out loud in a wide range of forums from a gathering of a few friends through to assemblies and special concerts. A great lift can be given to a school and to its work in poetry by the holding of a special event or concert which celebrates children's own poetic output alongside their response to the works of the poems they have been reading and learning in the ways presented above. One such event in Huntington C.P. School in Chester exemplifies the sort of occasion this can be and how it can be organised. This project, known as 'Miniatures', because of its focus on looking closely at small things, involved three classes in the school: the Reception, Year 1 and Year 2 class; the Year 3 class and the Year 6 class. A visual artist, Ian Douglas and a poet, Rose Flint, worked with these classes for two months.

In the latter stages of the project the children began to gather work together for a presentation. Much fruitful discussion took place – involving the class teachers, artist, poet and children – about which particular poems and pictures should be exhibited. Once decisions had been made the work itself was mounted. This process, too, was productive in terms of evaluating suitable ways of mounting. The children, particularly the older ones, were involved in a range of decision-making tasks with the aim of making their work prominent for the audience. Eventually, the drawings, paintings and poems were displayed in the foyer and school hall in a gallery-type exhibition. Every child had one poem and one drawing or painting in the display. Poems were all written in the children's own handwriting. This exhibition drew a good deal of attention on the night and in the days and weeks following. The children were proud of their exhibits and accompanied their parents to a viewing of the work after the concert.

The model for the concert was the well-polished, class-led assembly rather than a more formal occasion. It contained the following kinds of performance:

1. Small and large group choral recitations of poems learnt by heart.
2. Individual pupils from all three classes reading their own work.
3. A whole-class dance drama based on Ted Hughes's 'Spring Nature Notes' from the Year 6 class[18].
4. Musical settings of Patricia Hubbell's 'Shadows'[19] and the anonymous poem, 'I asked the little boy who cannot see. . . . .'[20] from the Year 3 class.
5. The artist and poet also talked to the audience about what they had tried to achieve in their work and attempted evaluations of it.

There was very much a family atmosphere, with the director of the project introducing each performance after the headteacher's general introduction. With the help of the artist, the children designed and circulated a programme to guests as they arrived. The guests were mainly the parents of children involved and governors, but were joined by the heads and liaison staff from the two secondary schools and a county councillor. Attendance of parents was very high and most expressed their pleasure with the evening's entertainment. The profile of poetry was considerably heightened, liaison with the high schools was seen to be about more than the transfer of formalities, and the children's parents had an insight into unfamiliar aspects of the curriculum.

The word 'publication' implies all forms of communicating a message to an audience, not only the production and dissemination of multiple copies of that message. However, if children are to experience a full process in their poetry work, it is imperative that they are involved in making multiple copies of their work as a way of completing the cycle of poetic activity. Although there has been a rise in this kind of activity in recent years, its full potential is generally not fully realised in schools.

For the simplest version of this I recall the production of an end of year collection of poems written by children in the small Shropshire primary school of Grafton C.P. with thirty-five pupils on its roll. Here, a group of Year 6 children, who were computer enthusiasts, were asked to set up the publication on a file in their class computer, then to invite all the children to come and type up the poems they thought were their best. By cutting and pasting they arranged the poems so that there was consistency in the spacing and subject-matter. The book was 'published' under the intriguing title, chosen by this 'committee', of 'Poems from out of this world' – almost a poem in itself with its implication of the ordinary and the extraordinary side by side. As parents and friends arrived for the final assembly of the school year they were given a copy.

In a school, a much more central use ought to be made of this act of publication. Several copies should be bound hard-back for the school library and classrooms and become part of the school's reading scheme. In my experience, such books 'of our own work' are highly popular and, over time, form a crucial link between past and present. Indeed, a tradition is established in such schools whereby a culture grows. Children coming to the school as infants quickly absorb the influences of the older ones in the school and one of these influences should be through the sharing of poetry.

The library or class collection of the children's own volumes of poetry is a rich resource for these youngsters to learn from and to emulate. In the larger picture, this is how cultures have been generated since time began. Just as our early ancestors would adopt the attitudes and stories from their elders through the singing of epics, chanting, riddle-telling and singing so, more modestly, may the latest generation of children entering a primary school learn from their elders and the previous generations of children and, of course, the works of the great poets of their own and other cultures. Books of children's poetry going back a number of years should sit on the library shelf side by side with, say, Ted Hughes's *Season Songs*, his joint anthology with Seamus Heaney: *The Rattle Bag*, and T. S. Eliot's *Old Possum's Book of Practical Cats*. Such a positive and enlightened statement as this bestows status on the children's work. This then further reinforces a notion which ultimately is as important as children's current levels of attainment: the sense that they are living members of a culture.

References.

1. Steiner, G. (11.1.98) Review in *The Observer* of Vendler, H. (1998) *The Art of Shakespeare's Sonnets*, Belknap, Harvard.
2. Ibid.
3. See Norman, K. (1992) *Thinking Voices*, Hodder and Stoughton, London.

4. See Britton, J. (1970) *Language and Learning*, Penguin, Harmondsworth.
5. See Barnes, D. (1976) *From Communication to Curriculum*, Penguin, Harmondsworth.
6. Bachelard (1969) *The Poetics of Reverie*, Beacon Press, Boston, USA.
7. Auden, W.H. (1954), *Secondary Worlds*, Faber, London.
8. Carter, D. (1994) *Imagined Worlds Project Report*, CPP, Mold.
9. Heaney, S. (1995) 'Feeling into Words', *The Redress of Poetry*, Faber, London.
10. Curnow, A. 'Wild Iron' in Heaney, S. and Hughes, T. (Eds) (1982) *The Rattle Bag*, Faber, London.
11. See Clegg, A.B. (Ed.) (1964) *The Excitement of Writing*, Chatto and Windus, London.
12. Ascribed to Clegg, A.B. Source unknown.
13. See, for instance, Brownjohn, S. (1980) *Does it have to rhyme?* Hodder and Stoughton, London.
14. Hughes, T. (1967) *Poetry in the Making*, Faber, London.
15. Ibid.
16. Ross, M. (1993) *Assessing Achievement in the Arts*, Open University Press, Buckingham.
17. Ibid.
18. Hughes, T. 'Spring Nature Notes' in (1976) *Season Songs*, Faber, London.
19. Hubbell, P. 'Shadows' in Summerfield, G. (Ed.) (1970) *Junior Voices* 1, Penguin, Harmondsworth.
20. Anonymous, 'I asked the little boy who cannot see . . . . .' in Harvey, A. (Ed.) (1991) *Shades of Green*, Julia MacRae Books, London.

Chapter Three

Planning, Assessment, Recording and Reporting

The making of choices

Teachers and student teachers are charged with responsibility for developing their children's affective, as well as their cognitive, abilities. In other words, the experiences which they provide must challenge the feelings as well as the intellects of pupils. In poetry this involves a complex set of choices. Teachers and student teachers need to choose poems which not only fit in with schemes of work, but which also contain within themselves what Seamus Heaney, in his essay 'Frontiers of Writing', calls 'a glimpsed alternative'.[1] So, the poems should not merely fulfil the needs of a topic but should be 'a source of truth' and a 'vehicle of harmony', to quote Heaney again.[2] They will carry other things to consider, not merely experiences directly relevant to the scheme, and the children will need to dwell in the poems for their own sakes as well as applying them directly to the subject matter of the topic. Poems must be fully explored, otherwise they are merely instruments for other goals.

A commitment to children's language development means that teachers cannot afford to choose poems which pander to lowest common denominators of taste. This is not to say that they rebuke children for their choices but that they base their own choices on a commitment to quality and wider notions of suitability and relevance, to what Marjorie Hourd called 'casting one's bread upon the water'.[3] Poems are relevant both to everyday life and to children's inner worlds of dreams, fears and hopes. They introduce new kinds of relevance, open up new alternatives. Too often teachers may take up poems in a hurry, simply because they relate to current topics. Proceeding in this way does a disservice both to children and to poetry and is to be avoided.

A fruitful way forward is for teachers and student teachers to build their own anthologies of high quality poems which are relevant to children in this fuller sense and which relate to a range of themes, including those in other parts of the curriculum. When looking for new poems teachers and student teachers might ask themselves the following initial questions:

1. Does it arouse my own curiosity and interest; does it delight me?
2. Is there originality in it or is it too derivative of other poems?
3. Does it create a new awareness within me; a different way of seeing things; does it transform the ordinary in some way?

If the poem cannot satisfy these things, it will be difficult to make it work for children.

For instance, let us say that a student on teaching practice, teaching a Year 4 class, is searching for poems to celebrate the arrival of spring, which will both appeal to the children and provide sufficient challenge for their intellectual curiosity. She comes across 'in Just-' by e.e.cummings[4] in an anthology. From the moment she reads the opening lines,

> in Just-
> spring   when the world is mud-
> luscious the little
> lame balloonman
>
> whistles   far   and wee
> and eddieandbill come
> running from marbles and
> piracies and it's
> spring
>
> when the world is puddle-wonderful

this student might well recognise something remarkable, a special quality which makes the poem valuable for the children she is teaching. Despite the idiosyncrasy of its punctuation and layout – e.e.cummings having fun on his typewriter – she might be strongly attracted to this poem. A first reading of the whole poem will immediately manifest its originality, its ability to generate fresh awareness of an old theme with its strange way of seeing. It does, indeed, transform the ordinary – children playing usual games and the visit of a familiar person – into the realm of dreams, into the extraordinary, even into myth. If she is a very practical student teacher, she will also see the richness of the poem's resources for developing her children's concepts through speaking and listening, for consolidating their growing knowledge of punctuation and for motivating them to emulate and write about their own experiences with a new freshness.

Teachers and students might make their choices using the model in the following simple diagram to guide them:

medium	message
vocabulary	stories
metaphors	feelings
sounds	ideas

If considered as a continuum, this provides a useful measure for beginning to make judgments about the nature of poems for classroom work. In certain poems the message is paramount and the medium's importance lies in how it strengthens that message. Much blank verse is like this. In other poems the medium is paramount and the message is 'absorbed' by it, so that the medium is virtually the message. Many nursery rhymes are like this. In most quality poems medium and message are integrated; the meanings of the words work through their textures, metaphors and patterns of sound. The words, the metaphors and the sounds point beyond the literal sense of the message, making poetry more intense and subtle than other kinds of writing.

In e.e.cummings's poem 'in Just-' the medium and message are integrated in this way. The story of the balloonman's visit is made memorable through the poem's way of presenting 'the world' he visits, which is 'mud-luscious'. It is also memorable for the strange little details about the balloonman himself with his plaintive whistle and his sensitively suggested handicap. This spare and lightly painted detail, so memorably put, is one example of why poetry is of such great value to children's education. It shows language not blowing its own trumpet as in many works of children's fiction, or ordering processions of fact as in non-fiction books. Language here is saying much by presenting a whole episode which is more extensive in its implications than in what is actually written. The poem demonstrates to children that language can be like a magnifying glass making the apparently unimportant details of the world stand out as significant and amazing.

A more extensive set of criteria for making judgments about the suitability of a poem for inclusion in an anthology is offered by this set of further questions for a student or teacher to ask:

1. The poet's mind and feelings: Will the poem make the children inquisitive? Can they relate personally to it? Will the ideas delight them? Are feelings such as comfort, excitement, sadness, joy, reflection, danger and fear honestly conveyed?
2. Richness of language: Will the sound of the words appeal to the children? Is the structure of lines accessible? Are the senses vividly evoked by the imagery, colour and tone? Is it sensuous? Will the rhythms carry them along? Do the similes/metaphors create new worlds which the children can enter?
3. Truth to life itself: Is ordinary experience transformed by the poem? Will it promote growth of knowledge about poetry and life? Will the children's language be developed? Will self-confidence in reading and responding to text be generated by it? Is it intellectually and emotionally challenging for the children?

These are important questions and such questioning will indicate a teacher's level of seriousness about the role of poetry in the curriculum. If poems are chosen willy-nilly, which often means choosing soft options from cheap pulp anthologies, vital opportunities may be blown. At a time when poetry has to hold its place in the queue for inclusion in classroom work, such squandered opportunities will damage the status of poetry in children's perceptions. They may think, like a class of children recently observed, that poetry is merely words that make you laugh and no more enlightening than the latest 'Ha, ha, ha bump!' joke book.

So, for instance, another student teacher looking for a poem about animals to share with her Year 6 class might raise her expectations high when she reads David Wevill's translation from the Hungarian of Ferenc Juhasz's 'The Birth of the Foal' in her copy of *The Rattle Bag*. When reading such lines as

> **As May was opening the rosebuds,**
> **elder and lilac beginning to bloom,**
> **it was time for the mare to foal.**

and

> **Dawn bounced up in a bright red hat,**
> **waved at the world and skipped away.**
> **Up staggered the foal . . . . .**[5]

with their easy mixing of metaphor and realism, our student teacher might perceive the life-enhancing qualities in such a poem and feel it just right for her Year 6 class. If she uses it she will activate the children's curiosities and feelings powerfully. In this poem, of which these lines are typical, the very thing that attracts children to young animals is presented in a transformative way. All children, even the hardest playground bullies, love the cuddly, the vulnerable and the cute. This group of feelings can so easily drift into sentimentality and fail to grow further. This poem, and many like it, offers the possibility of genuine growth here. So tenderly, yet so strongly, is the story told and its challenge is not only to the child's sense of a creature's vulnerability. Juhasz contextualises it in a way which gives it cosmic importance. Somehow, the very heavens bless the moment of the foal's birth and dawn celebrates it by gambolling about and waving. The strength of this context is in such details, within a metaphorical framework, which bestow a human kind of consciousness onto the inanimate.

Even though this is a translation, our student will surely be excited by a poetic language which is challengingly rich and sensuous at the same time as being so accessible and witty. She will find in Juhasz's poem that a common event – the birth of an animal – is transformed into a glorious affirmation of life. Maybe she will see the gains for her children in terms of intellectual challenge, psychological growth and emotional satisfaction. Here is a poem to heal and enhance the children's very sense of life. In making such speculations I may be idealising our imaginary student, but they indicate the real possibilities behind the current interest in 'high expectations' of children in schools.

Aims and organisation

Obviously, any school's policy statement, progression statements and schemes of work for poetry will appear in its English policy document. Here, I intend to provide sentences and paragraphs for poetry which teachers can adapt when either writing for the first time or revising their school's English documentation. They may appear a little too long, but can be refined to fit in with the other statements for English. Any policy document will begin with aims and there follows a set for poetry.

The aims for poetry are to develop every child's:

- imagination and inventiveness with words;
- knowledge and enjoyment of poetic language and forms, and of poets from a range of cultures and periods;
- ability to listen acutely and sensitively to readings of poetry;
- ability to read poetry with increasing understanding and empathy;
- ability to speak poetry with increasing clarity and expression;
- knowledge of, and ability to respond to, a growing canon of poetry;
- ability as a writer of poetry in a range of forms;
- skills of presentation, exhibition and publication of finished works.

It is also normal in contemporary documentation to state the teaching and learning strategies that will be adopted to pursue the aims, as follows. The children will:

- listen to teachers, each other, poets and visitors reading poetry;
- speak and sing poems and songs learnt by heart, and read out loud;
- read poetry as part of the development of their reading skills and for developing reading as a leisure activity;
- learn poetry by heart for a variety of classroom and whole school performances and learn the names of poets and the contexts of their work;
- learn meanings in poems and knowledge of poetic forms by conversing in small and large groups, and participate in classroom 'poetry conferences';
- explore the meanings in poems by responding to them in dance, drama, music, visual art and writing;
- compose their own poems orally and, increasingly, through writing;
- Perform, exhibit and publish their work in magazines for others to share.

The logic of the current planning system is to outline the classroom organisation and management implied by the teaching and learning strategies, as follows:

- classrooms and other parts of the school to have poetry corners, where the children have the time, space and quietness to 'stand and stare';
- the ready availability of poetry books, posters and individual poems (including children's own work) in these corners;
- availability of a large space (school hall) for dance, drama and musical responses to poetry; also for presentations involving poetry and the rehearsals necessary to prepare for them;
- availability of practical areas for responses to poetry through art;
- equality of opportunity in terms of access to a range of resources to suit all abilities, genders and ethnic backgrounds; a canon of available poetry drawn from many parts of the world with a wide range from the simplest nursery rhymes through to mature works of great world poets; and the consideration that all children are poets in their own right, however modest their current works might be;

● cross curricular approaches so that poetry will not only be experienced as a literary form but also will be used in topic and project work; this usage will be sensitively managed to preserve the integrity of the poems used.

The learning objectives for a scheme of work

A scheme of work for poetry can successfully be developed out of the aims, strategies and organisation, using the following learning objectives. Each objective has suggested activities and examples for Key Stage 1 and Key Stage 2, designed to encompass most Attainment Targets in National Curriculum English. The learning objectives are as follows. Children should be taught:

1. To use imagination actively in a range of situations.
   a) Recall and talk about dreams they have had.
   b) Listen to recorded sounds/music and imagine where they are, what is there, what it is like to be there, the colours, light/dark, feelings.
   KS1 example: Debussy's 'La Mer'.
   KS2 example: Stravinsky's 'The Rite of Spring'.
   c) Present fairy tale or mythical images or ideas and the pupils say what they are like, their colours, relationship, what happens.
   KS1: king, forest, magic bird.
   KS2: god, hero, quest, magic ring, monster.
   d) Present evocative lines from poems and ask them to 'see it' then describe what they saw.
   KS1: 'Nimbletail flies up the oak' from 'The Intruder' by James Reeves.
   KS2: 'The sedge has wither'd from the lake' from Keats's 'La Belle Dame Sans Merci'.
   e) Tell/read a fairy tale or myth and at various moments ask them to tell you what they see, feel, hear, smell, imagine.
   KS1: Hansel and Gretel abandoned in the woods.
   KS2: Theseus in the labyrinth.
   f) Show them an evocative painting or drawing and ask them to describe what they would see, feel, hear, smell and do if they went into the picture.
   KS1: 'Impression Sunrise' by Claude Monet.
   KS2: 'The Field of Mars' by Marc Chagall.

2. To be playful and adventurous with words and phrases.
   a) Draw attention of class to, and record, any interesting/strange/funny/ambiguous things individuals say or write in contexts other than poetry.
   KS1: "Miss, look at my sand sausage roll."
   KS2: "I hurt the little ditch behind my knee."
   b) Play word games in which children follow each other in providing rhyming, alliterating, similar-sounding or opposite-sounding words and phrases. Children draw, or act/move like, or make the sound of, each variation of the sound.
   KS1: "Mouse: brown mouse, town mouse, clown mouse, drowned mouse."

KS2: "Tree: trapped in a tree; troublesome tree; the roof was trashed by a tree; trembling branches of a tree in a tender breeze; tree dressed in her trim spring gown."

c) Whenever interesting new words or phrases are encountered, ask "What could that mean?" rather than merely telling the children what they mean. Much fun is to be had distorting the meaning of sentences using the wrong answers, rather than dismissing them as "wrong".

KS1: Science – Light source. "Does it mean something not very heavy to put on your chips?"

KS2: Geography – Supply of goods: "Are they supplied to fight the bads?"

d) Play 'make-up-a-word' games.

KS1: holly leaf is 'ickypokey' holly leaf.

KS2: the van making deliveries to the kitchen is the 'wumfing-weeching-kludding' van that brings 'scrompy-champy-golpy grub' to the kitchen.

e) Play 'make-a-new-name' games.

KS1: after experiencing a dead teasel plant through the senses, children call it 'prickle-fist', 'busby-head', 'long tall poky-top', 'scraper'.

KS2: after doing a topic based on a local patch of wasteland, children make new names based on knowledge of it: 'beetle-wiggly-hideout'; 'two-dip-spot-with-a-bump'; 'death-trap-alley'.

f) Feature nicknames and establish nicknames for every member of the class with the opportunity to change them if something new happens to the child.

KS1: child who falls off her bike in the nettles is nicknamed 'Fell-in-nettles'or 'Pinky-bump-skin'.

KS2: child who finds it difficult to listen before speaking himself is nicknamed: 'The Interrupter', 'Tongue-in-a-hurry' or 'Who-burns-to-chat'.

g) Ten minute 'tell-a-joke' sessions, children to make their own jokes up. Feature joke-books, collect cracker jokes. Focus on jokes that depend on ambiguities in words and talk about this aspect of jokes with older pupils.

KS1: "Knock, knock, who's there?" jokes.

KS2: 'What do you get if you cross . . .' jokes.

h) Encourage the recognition and practice of playing on the potential meanings of words.

KS1: 'Shaun' the sheep from Wallace and Gromit's 'A Close Shave'.

KS2: 'Subtraction': could also mean 'underneath the wheel of an engine'.

3. To know and enjoy a growing body of poetic language and forms; and

4. To know and enjoy the work of a growing number of poets, past and present, in English and translated from other cultures.

a) Listen to, learn by heart and recite, chant or sing (i) English nursery rhymes, action poems, song lyrics, poems; (ii) extracts or complete classic poems; (iii) poems from other cultures.

KS1: (i) 'Midnight Forest', Judith Nicholls. (ii) 'The Snare', James Stephens. (iii) 'The

Door', Miroslav Holub; 'Omen', Birago Diop.

KS2: (i) 'Roman Wall Blues', Auden. (ii) 'Full fathom five thy father lies/Of his bones are coral made', Shakespeare; 'Kubla Khan', Coleridge. (iii) 'A Withered Tree', Han Yu.

b) Use extracts from a range of poetic forms and different poetic phrases as part of displays.

KS1: 'tiny fish/Quick little splinters of life', D. H. Lawrence – placed near fishtank or pond.

KS2: 'They lean over the path,/Adder-mouthed', Theodore Roethke – placed near flowers.

c) Encounter poems in reading scheme material, with the time for re-reading and sharing.

KS1: 'Fog', Carl Sandburg; 'The Duck', Ogden Nash.

KS2: 'Wild Iron', Allen Curnow; 'Hide and Seek', Walter de la Mare.

d) Special focus weeks on poetry from other cultures or include in Geography projects.

KS1: A John Agard week.

KS2: 'Poems from India' or a 'Poems from Round the World' week.

5. To listen acutely and sensitively to readings of poetry by teachers, other pupils and visitors.

a) Teacher reads poem at the end of a session just for enjoyment, or to introduce new topic, or as part of sequence of poetry lessons.

b) Favourites: individually or in groups children prepare and read poems to the class, to include sometimes a special focus as above (4d), or a theme such as animals.

c) Readings in assemblies, services, concerts.

d) Poetry exchanges: teachers read favourites to each other's classes.

e) Poet in residence reads own work.

f) Students and other visitors invited to read favourite poems.

6. To read poetry with understanding.

a) Read poems and talk about them to teacher and friends.

b) Select poems individually and in groups for use in topics.

c) Review poems both orally and in writing.

d) Recommend poems to others.

7. To read poetry with empathy.

a) Choosing poems in which people's or animals' feelings are expressed.

KS1: 'Behold', Mary Kawena Pukui.

KS2: 'The Snare', James Stephens.

b) Talking about the feelings in selected poems.

KS1: John Clare's feelings for the wagtail in 'Little Trotty Wagtail'.

KS2: Gerard Manley Hopkins' feelings in 'Inversnaid'.

c) Talking or writing about being the poet or character.
KS1: What would it be like to be unable to see colours?' after reading 'I asked the little boy who cannot see', Anonymous.
KS2: The Roman wall soldier in 'Roman Wall Blues', W. H. Auden.

8. To recite poems and sing songs clearly and with expression.
   a) In groups children decide how to recite poems then practise reciting them.
   KS1: 'Overheard on a Saltmarsh', Harold Monro.
   KS2: Carl Sandburg's 'Old Deep Sing-Song'.
   b) Sharings in class with discussion about best ways of reciting the lines.
   KS1: 'Wild with the iron that tears at the nail/And the foundering shriek of the gale' from 'Wild Iron', Allen Curnow.
   KS2: 'A windpuff-bonnet of fawn froth/Turns and twindles over the broth' from 'Inversnaid' by G. M. Hopkins.

9. To know several important poems and songs by heart.
   a) Learning set poems and songs connected with other school work and reciting them individually, in groups and as a class.
   KS1: 'Fog', Carl Sandburg, for topic work on weather.
   KS2: Auden's 'Roman Wall Blues', for History project on Romans.
   b) Learning poems as part of reading programmes.
   KS1: 'Hide and Seek', Walter de la Mare, for repetition.
   KS2: 'Spell of Creation', Kathleen Raine, for clear progression of ideas.
   c) Learning favourite poems to share with others.
   d) Learning poems and songs for special events in the life of the school.

10. To take part in discussing poetry with others.
    a) Joining in class discussions led by the teacher.
    b) Discussing poems directly with the teacher, other adults or older children.
    c) Joining in organised group discussions with classmates.
    KS1: Work out who 'Two-boots', 'Nimbletail' *et al.* are in 'The Intruder', James Reeves.
    KS2: Decide what is wrong with the 'knight at arms' in Keats' 'La Belle Dame Sans Merci'.

11. To explain and describe a poem to the teacher and other children.
    a) As part of readings, explain a poem to a classmate, to the teacher, to other adults, or older children.
    b) Making formal presentations, including recitations, to groups, the whole class, other classes or the whole school.

12. To respond to poetry through dance, drama, art, music and writing.
    a) Whole class led by the teacher explore poems through one or a combination of dance, drama, art, music and new writing.

KS1: Imagining about what is behind the door in 'The Door', Miroslav Holub.

KS2: Imagining Xanadu in 'Kubla Khan', Coleridge.

b) Individuals work out ideas for developing poems in dance, drama, art, music or writing.

KS1: Painting what was seen in 'There I saw', Anonymous.

KS2: Painting 'Above the Dock', T. E. Hulme.

c) Groups make dances, plays, pictures or sculptures, tunes or sound effects or new writing.

KS1: Enacting the encounter between the nymph and the goblin in 'Overheard on a Saltmarsh', Harold Monro, adding new ideas and lines to it.

KS2: Making the sounds, the body and the movements of the Loch Ness monster in 'The Loch Ness Monster's Song', Edwin Morgan.

13. To perform responses to poetry in dance, drama and music.

Pieces of dance, drama and music, explored (Objective 12) in response to poetry, demonstrated, or rehearsed then performed to other classes.

KS1: A concert of several performance items: dance ('There I saw', Anonymous), drama ('Overheard on a Saltmarsh', Harold Monro) and sound tracks ('Wild Iron', Allen Curnow)

KS2: Dance-drama with composed music and improvised drama of Coleridge's 'Kubla Khan'.

14. To develop responses to poetry in art into finished works.

a) Ideas from exploratory sessions developed into finished works after discussion with teacher, mounted and displayed for others to see.

b) Larger scale projects.

KS1: A series of paintings to tell the story of how the nymph acquired the beads in 'Overheard on a Saltmarsh', Harold Monro.

KS2: A large-scale mural of Xanadu from Coleridge's 'Kubla Khan'.

15. To compose poetry orally and in writing both in free and structured forms.

a) Spontaneous poetic ideas recorded on audiotape or written down as poems.

b) Make a class poem: each child provides one line on a set theme.

c) Record on tape/write responses to sounds and music (Objective 1b), fairy tale images (1c), evocative lines (1d), moments in fairy tales (1e) and pictures (1f).

d) Record on tape/write responses to invented words and names (Objectives 2d and 2e).

e) Recall a dream and write it as a poem rather than a story.

f) Take the 'mind on a walk' then write the walk as a poem.

g) Engage with a poem of the pure imagination and add new images and ideas to it or imitate its format to write on a different theme.

h) Engage with a natural or man-made object and write as poem.

i) Engage with a place through the senses and write as poem.

j) Observe happenings and human/animal behaviour and write as poem.

k) Engage with works of literature and make poems in response.

16. To present compositions in handwriting, print and recitation.
    a) Draft and redraft poems written in activities above (15 a-k).
    b) Copy out final draft paying due attention to letter formation, joins, design and layout. Mount for display on wall or in class or personal books.
    c) Word-process final draft, paying attention to format, font, size and style. Present in appropriate way for readers.
    d) Prepare and rehearse recitation of copied/word-processed poem.

17. To take part in the exhibition of compositions and responses to poetry in visual art.
    a) Mount own work after discussion with teacher.
    b) Help in decision-making about overall arrangement of exhibition.
    c) Hand-write or word-process captions and labels for the mounts.
    d) Guide visitors around the exhibition, explaining the various pieces of work.

18. To take part in the publication of compositions.
    a) Help make class books and mount poems in them.
    b) Make own books, mount poems in them and display.
    c) Help compile word-processed anthology of own and others' poems and produce multiple copies for distribution.
    d) Help edit, promote and distribute poetry magazine.

Assessing children's poetry-making

Assessing children's writing is fraught with difficulties and most teachers and Ofsted inspectors find the levelling of pupils' written work an imprecise activity. In the end we have to admit that personal opinion will inevitably play a part and that judgements will be contestable.

The mass of children's written work which is levelled in schools each year is heavily weighted towards versions of prose, which is easier to assess than poetry. Indeed, prose is what was in the minds of the designers of the levels in the English orders, and if we look at the standard assessment tasks for writing at both key stages all the tasks test children's abilities in prose-writing. Teachers can, therefore, be forgiven if they interpret these signals as meaning that prose has greater status than poetry when developing children's writing skills. The making of poetry is far more difficult to assess and is possibly one of the reasons it was omitted from the Level Descriptions in the English orders.

This, however, is an unacceptable situation and does not square with statements about poetry in the Programmes of Study and in the National Literacy Strategy 'Framework'. (NLS) To assume its rightful status alongside prose, poetry must be assessed as objectively as possible. Otherwise, it becomes acceptable to consider poetry-making as a fringe activity, a sort of occasional pursuit when the real work is finished, with teachers accepting and praising anything the children produce – a patronising attitude.

I offer here a set of level descriptions for the making of poetry, which will later be applied to actual pieces of children's poetry. In creating these levels I have four parameters: the National Curriculum English Writing levels which already exist; the need to recognise the quality of children's ideas when they make poetry; children's developing use of aspects of poetic form; and – implicit in the National Curriculum levels – the child's development of independence in writing. This obviously leads to a compromise and opens the prospect of differences of opinion. A piece of work might be stronger according to one set of criteria than the other. Here we simply have to make an honest judgement according to our experience.

So, bearing in mind the compromises that are being made when we make judgements about children's poems, here is a set of Level Descriptions intended to supplement those in the English orders of the National Curriculum document:

English: Poetry-Making Level Descriptions
Level 1:
Able to use imagination.
Some trace of poetic feature: rhythm, rhyme, alliteration, colour in use of vocabulary, figurative language, metaphor and simile.
Level 2:
Increasing use of imagination.
Clearly discernible poetic features.
Level 3:
Confident use of imagination and some originality.
Poetic phrases and lines are created.
Level 4:
Shows some originality in creating poetic ideas.
Well-structured verses, passages or short forms created.
Level 5:
Shows flair in creating poetic ideas.
Increasing control over poetic form.
Level 6:
Summons poetic ideas quickly and uses them effectively.
Creates well-structured, original and effective whole poems.

Such level descriptions mean little unless we see them applied to actual pieces of children's work. Here, with a little background to each piece of work, are six children's poems which are levelled according to the descriptions above:

> *Level 1:*
> Cheetah growling at the snow
> and the thunderstorm came
> and the birds flew
> and the cheetah ran away.
> The snake looked at the birds
> and he stung the thunderstorm
> so it went away.

This poem was written by Wesley in emergent writing during a session on animals in bad weather on a Clwyd Poetry Project pilot. Its outstanding strength is the quality of the child's imagination which makes the snake take revenge on the threatening clouds. It was by a four-year-old child and was formless, apart from the sense of metaphor in a snake stinging a thunderstorm. The writing could not be understood and the child had to tell the visiting poet what the writing meant. The compromise here is between the strong quality of the poetic ideas and a weakness in the other three parameters, which is to be expected from one so young.

Level 2:
It was a silver light that glowed
like the moon, a golden eagle
waiting by the window.
I went down like a feather.
I looked in the mirror.
I saw something staring
then an eagle came in shining like snow.
Lights on the wall with glass
triangles shining, a remote-control
car, a tiny wood figure. Lassie
my dog scratching at the door.

This poem was written on another Clwyd Poetry Project pilot by six-year-old Emma and needed work on spelling and punctuation. She wrote quite independently in response to a task set by the visiting poet. The child's imagination is stimulated, which leads to original ideas. Some aspects of form are quite strong, such as the vivid similes and sense of rhythm.

Level 3:
'To the tower'
Up the bottle-top steps
we wind with cobwebs
that are at one end and flies
that have had their end in the cobwebs,
then again comes the spider
out of his hiding place,
then gone are the flies.
Down from the tower.
Wind down unscrewing
the bottle-tops as they go wider
and at the end the door is
like the top of the bottle-opener.

This, by ten-year-old Robina, was written during a visit to the tower of the local church. Robina had difficulties with her literacy, was receiving specialist help for it, and the poem was deficient in spelling and punctuation. However, her metaphor for the spiral staircase – a bottle-top – is delightfully original and very well developed in the second part of the poem with the door as the bottle-opener. The strengths of the poem are the originality of its overall concept based around a metaphor, which is well developed. The weaknesses are technical ones involving spelling and punctuation.

> *Level 4:*
> 'Under a leaf'
> Under a leaf
> left from last year
> there could be anything there.
> An army of ants
> busy building a town
> or a fat slimy toad
> pulsing up and down.
> Maybe a lizard
> quick and red
> or a little mouse
> curled up in its bed.
> Under a leaf
> left from last year
> there could be anything,
> anything there.

The strength of this poem, written by Iwan, a Year 5 child, is its verse structure with a successful use of rhyme, not easy for primary children. Iwan displays some originality in the proposal that such a range of creatures might be found underneath a leaf. The piece was written independently and required very little assistance from the teacher. It was written with few technical errors.

> *Level 5:*
> 'Wasp's Nest'
> Deserted with a cold chill of winter.
> Showing evidence of dooms.
> Old compartments filled with
> the bitterness of death.
> Going dry and dying,
> Cracking into splinters,
> also people kick and spoil
> the delicate formation.
> But spring comes and the nest recovers
> and new wasps come and start their living.

This piece, by eleven-year-old David, was written independently in very good cursive script and with only a few spelling mistakes, during a lesson in which several activities were taking place. Its quality is the sureness of touch with which the child turns the old wasps' nest into words. Some lines cannot be bettered: 'Deserted with a cold chill of winter' and 'Old compartments filled with the bitterness of death', for instance. In such lines the child has transformed an object on a classroom table into a subtle metaphorical concept in which winter is almost animate and seems deliberately to bring bitterness. The poem is also strong for the subtle colouring of the vocabulary in such phrases as 'the delicate formation' and 'Going dry and dying'. Figurative language is used with accomplishment, although some parts are stronger than others.

> *Level 6:*
> 'The stealer'
> The butterfly hovered
> over the hawthorn pollen
> Robbing the bush
> of her sweet scent.
> Night black streaks
> are strewn on orange wings
> Which dip and flutter
> on the diving wind.

This very nearly perfect child poem was written by ten-year-old Fiona during her Whit holidays. The only influence over her was that she had worked for many months with a poetry-loving teacher, who had suggested that his class might like to write some poems while they were off school. It required no corrections and was written in flawless cursive script. The whole conception in this poem is metaphorical from the title itself – which postulates that the butterfly is a thief – to the 'diving wind' which joins the butterfly's wings 'which dip and flutter' in that spring dance. Its structure is immaculate, its figurative language beautifully and delicately coloured in such phrases as 'Night black streaks' for the markings on the wings. There is a strong sense of a complete and highly effective poem here.

The literacy hour and beyond

Many teachers in England are undergoing or have undergone training for the new literacy strategy and, in particular, for the implementation of the literacy hour. Many of the fears for poetry in the primary school so far expressed in this book will be realised if those teachers are coralled into a mainly instrumental use of texts rather than honouring the integrity of the texts in the activities they subsequently set for children. This instrumentality appears – on the surface – to be obvious in the NLS's structure for the literacy hour. This seems to be entirely analytical of texts and concerned only with what a text can furnish in terms of performance skills in reading and writing and knowledge about language. There could develop a sense of the isolatedness of the skills and the knowledge from the pursuit of meaning in literature and the intellectual and emotional growth which is the ultimate aim of reading and writing.

The National Literacy Strategy is already being seen as making a serious challenge to teachers, schools and educational authorities at the time of writing of this book (spring 1998). Millions of pounds are being committed to the response with new literacy consultants appointed by almost every local education authority. Many teachers are fearful of yet another set of expectations being foisted upon them after ten years of having to respond to new initiatives from the government of the day.

I have already made my position clear in terms of the dangers to the status of poetry in the primary school inherent in this particular initiative. As with the National Curriculum orders for English themselves, poetry may easily get lost. Yet with the challenge, with the dangers, come opportunities, as is often the case. These opportunities may be seized by those with the commitment and craft to make the initiative work for the greater cause of children's intellectual and emotional growth through literature. This section of the book, therefore, is at the heart of my effort to realise my own commitment to poetry in the primary school and my craft in finding ways to do so. It appears to me now that, if used wisely, the literacy hour can form the basis of a deeper engagement with poetry and I hope to prove that here.

The most contentious element in the literacy hour proposals is that texts will be used as exemplars for the teaching of phonics and spelling, punctuation, grammar and sentence structure. Yet, even here, there are opportunities for the advancement of children's experience and understanding of poetry. Essentially, this is about analysis of texts and there is nothing wrong with that even with a class of four-year-olds, providing that the poem is primarily experienced in its *wholeness*. Then, analysis does not cut up for cutting up's sake. Analysis actually serves to enhance the experience of the poem in its wholeness. It is the same with literary criticism for students in the sixth form or university. If the work is immediately subject to the critic's knife then many students will lose interest. However, if the student enters the world of the work, experiences it emotionally as well as intellectually, then an essay, say, by T. S. Eliot or George Steiner can actually add to the emotion and meaning of that work.

Let us look at this in application to the literacy hour at either end of the key stages of the primary school. The poem, 'Storm', which is suggested in the section of lessons for Reception children below (Chapter Four), provides opportunities for developing their ability to recognise and say the sounds which a variety of letters make in a context. This makes it very useful for developing phonic and spelling skills. However, if this teaching is carried out within a context in which the poem is spoken chorally and actually performed to audiences, then the very pursuit of its phonics will enhance the children's awareness of and ability to communicate its pattern of sounds. The one aim benefits the other and the overall experience is multiplied. The phonic learning will be made more memorable because of the experience of choral speaking and, maybe, exploration through the arts. The speaking of it will be more accurate and precise because of the close focus on the exact sounds the letters make.

Let us look more closely at this argument. When looking at the words in 'Storm' the final sound '-all' will be seen as a key feature because it provides the poem's rhyme scheme, 'Wild winds/call, call/Rain, hail/fall, fall/Fresh gales/squall, squall./Tossed trees/tall, tall/Crash down/all, all.' This will provide much of the words work in the lesson. The children will live with that sound chiming in their ears. It will be the poem's key feature for them and will help them recognise that sound every time they encounter it in their reading and writing. They will say it more clearly and with more emphasis, also, because they have dwelt with it so much.

However, because the children are so young and learning to read and write at an elementary level, they will also focus on the beginning letter-sounds of every word (w, c, r, h, f, fr, g, squ, t, tr, cr, d), all the long and short vowel sounds (short – i in 'wind', e in 'fresh', a in 'crash', o in 'tossed'; long – i in 'wild', ai in 'rain', a in 'call', a in 'gales', ow in 'down') and all the final letter-sounds (-ld, -nds, -ll, -n, -l, -sh, -s, -ed). They will work on saying sounds such as the difficult 'squ-','-nds', and '-ld' so that when they need to say 'squall, squall', 'winds' and 'wild' they will pronounce those words more clearly. So the analysis has double value. It develops the children's formal literacy skills and it develops their awareness of and ability to make the sounds of poetry.

In their analytical work, Key Stage 2 children will focus not only on words and sentences but also more specifically on poetic features. Here again the analytical work can enhance the children's appreciation of the poem itself. In 'The Birth of the Foal', which I would suggest as suitable for Year 6 children, a key aspect is the poet Ferenc Juhasz's use of personification. Therefore, after experiencing the poem as a whole through choral speech and discussion, the children may explore those words, phrases and sentences which are literal and those which are figurative, largely through personification as in the lines quoted earlier: 'Dawn bounced up in a bright red hat/waved at the world and skipped away/Up staggered the foal . . . . .' A task might be set here, in which groups sort out the literal from the figurative simply by underlining, as demonstrated. Such an exercise will reveal that in some poems it is not so much the rhythms, rhymes, alliteration and other sound features where the poetry is found, as in its metaphorical dimension. This will be the main analytical concern for this particular poem.

However, much can also be revealed about the nature of the poem's 'world' through the apparently more mundane listing of examples of its key parts of speech. For instance, a listing of the poem's adjectives, such as 'bone-tired', 'heavy-bellied', 'glue-blind', 'soft' and 'golden', would reveal that there are not many (nine altogether) compared to the number of nouns (forty-nine). Children might then be led to realise that this is because much of the description in the poem is provided by the metaphors through personification. In one of the other verses Juhasz personifies the hay as being asleep rather than describing the night as being quiet ('when even the hay slept'). Such considerations are crucial to any child's understanding of what poetry essentially is. Yet such an exercise also hits the target of developing children's knowledge of parts of speech in a memorable way.

In Chapter Four of the book I demonstrate what a poetry literacy hour can look like in all year groups of the primary school. There are lesson sequences covering a week's work for each of these age groups. These are written for teachers and students both to try as they stand or to adapt for other year groups, themes and poems. This chapter then shows how the close focus of the literacy hour itself can be used to develop work in the arts of music, drama, dance and visual art. This is of equal importance as it will provide children with the experience of pursuing the expressive aspects of particular poems and broaden their perspectives. The section begins with a summary of the structure of a literacy hour.

References

1. Heaney, S. (1994) 'Frontiers of Writing', *The Redress of Poetry*, Faber, London.
2. Ibid.
3. Hourd, M.L. (1949) *The Education of the Poetic Spirit*, Heinemann, London.
4. cummings, e.e. (1953) 'in Just-' in *Tulips and chimneys*, Liveright, New York.
5. Juhasz, F., translated by Wevill, D. 'The Birth of the Foal' in Heaney, S. and Hughes, T. (Eds.) (1984) *The Rattle Bag*, Faber, London.

Chapter Four

Literacy Hour Lessons

Interpreting the NLS's Framework

The National Literacy Strategy's (NLS) 'Framework for Teaching' is promoting an approach to the development of literacy based upon a daily hour of intensive activity. A format for lessons has been devised, which divides the hour into four areas of activity. At Key Stage 1 the hour is conceived as follows:

1. Whole class teaching for approximately 15 minutes in which texts are shared in a balance of reading and writing.
2. Whole class teaching for approximately 15 minutes in which the focus is on the words in the text.
3. Group activities of approximately 20 minutes in which children engage in independent reading, writing or word work activities. The teacher is supposed to work with each group twice a week with a focus on guided text work. The groups are supposed to be setted.
4. Whole class teaching for approximately 10 minutes in which work is reviewed, reflected upon and presented.

At Key Stage 2 the hour is conceived similarly but with a few minor differences as follows:

1. Whole class teaching for approximately 15 minutes in which texts are shared in a balance of reading and writing.
2. Whole class teaching for approximately 15 minutes in which the focus is on the words in the text and the structure of sentences.
3. Group activities of approximately 20 minutes in which children engage in independent reading, writing or word work activities. The teacher is supposed to work with each group once a week with a focus on guided text work. The groups are supposed to be setted.
4. Whole class teaching for approximately 10 minutes in which work is reviewed, reflected upon and presented.[1]

The basic pattern here is straightforward for both Key Stage 1 and 2 and can easily accommodate good poetry teaching at the same time as it develops children's literacy skills. Its problems are that children will have to be moved on from one activity to another when, perhaps, they are already fruitfully involved. However, if a poetry project is thought of in terms of a week's work, children should be able to pick up where they left off the following day. I, therefore, offer the following interpretation as a model of good practice in such a literacy hour:

1. The lesson starts with teacher and children engaging with the same text, and the quality of that text is vital. It should be chosen using the sort of criteria discussed above, rather than merely because it serves the purpose identified using literacy hour criteria alone. This text I shall call the **prime text**. Much will depend on the quality of the interaction between teacher and class over the prime text at this early stage of the lesson. If enthusiasm and excitement are not generated here, the rest of the lesson and unit of work may become lifeless and boring. So, the teacher must practise reading the prime text before representing it to the children. Even before this lesson it would be advisable for the children to have the opportunity to start learning the poem by heart at home. (See below for advice on this.)

2. After 15 minutes or so the focus will shift onto key words in the text and, at Key Stage 2, on sentence and/or verse structures in it. What the 'Framework' implies here is the development firstly of phonic and spelling skills, then of knowledge of punctuation and grammar, in addition to the children's understanding of the texts as a whole. In a poem there will be the further need to develop children's awareness then knowledge of poetic features such as rhythm, rhyme, alliteration and metaphor. Obviously, there is enormous overlap between both of these needs. Poetic features such as rhyme are a key aid to children's memories of phonics and spelling in particular. For the specific targeting of some of these skills I provide in the examples other poems or extracts. These I call **support texts**.

3. Half an hour into the lesson the children shift again, this time onto group work. They engage in reading and writing tasks based on the prime text, on written work or word work. The 'Framework' recommends here that children be setted by ability. Many teachers, however, will feel that literacy objectives can be achieved without resorting to setting. In the examples that follow I provide material which can be used for both approaches. These examples will involve children in reading prime texts, writing their own poems, creatively conversing and, particularly in the 'tasks for sets', reading new poems on the same themes as the main texts. These new poems I will call **secondary texts**.

4. Finally, ten minutes before the end of the lesson, the children gather as a class to review, reflect and present work. One of the weaknesses in this model is the short amount of time made available for this valuable activity. Here, I presume that teachers will follow a poetry unit of literacy hours for a week or fortnight and, if this is the case and they are wise, they will keep this section of each lesson to a brief five minute summary. The time can then be saved up for the last session so that children have greater opportunity for presentations. If the children have been engaged in cross-curricular arts work then a sharing event outside of the literacy hour should be arranged.

The literacy hour and the Clwyd Poetry Project model

At this point it will be valuable to examine the common ground which exists between the Clwyd Poetry Project (CPP) ways of working and the NLS 'Framework'. In the following chart the CPP's ways of working are represented in italics:

1. Sharing the text using reading and writing: *listening, speaking, reading, memorising.* (*Writing* means note-taking here.)
2. Focus on key words in the text and, at Key Stage 2, focus on sentence and/or verse structures in the text: *reading, creatively conversing.*
3. Pupils engaged in reading based on the text or extension texts, written work or word work: *reading, creatively conversing, composing.*
4. Reviews, reflections and presentations: *presenting.*

Any responses to prime texts made through work in the arts of music, dance, drama and art, which involve further presentations, as discussed above, involve expressively engaging and presenting.

The success of the interpretation which I am promoting here will be greatly advanced by children memorising prime texts. With the current pressure on the primary curriculum this may only be fully realised if teachers organise their children to take home copies of the texts for learning during the weekend before the poetry literacy lessons begin.

These texts should be sent with a letter to parents suggesting ways to help their children as follows:

- Read the poem to your child while he/she follows it with a finger.
- Read the poem with your child, both following the lines with your fingers.
- Child reads the poem to you and you gently correct any mistakes.
- You hold the poem so that your child cannot see it. Then read a line and ask your child to repeat it and go through the whole poem several times like this until your child is getting better at repeating the lines.
- Ask child to read the poem, then to give it to you while he/she tries to say all of it off by heart. Every time your child gets stuck, prompt him/her immediately.
- Continue this process until your child knows the poem off by heart.

The aim is to get all of the children with a fairly good recall of the poem before the first lesson on the Monday morning. The literacy work will then have the boost of everybody being familiar with the text and having plenty of curiosity about it.

Preparing for and conducting a poetry literacy hour

When preparing for a poetry literacy hour teachers and students need to do the following:

- Practise reading the various texts, concentrating on phrasing, expression and accuracy so that the appeal of the material is fully communicated to the children.
- Make poster versions of the prime text and support texts.

- Make flash cards of any blends, individual words or phrases to be developed.
- Provide every child with a smaller version of the poem for group work.
- Provide a notepad/exercise book and pen/pencil for every child. This will need to be used throughout the literacy hour, particularly with older children.
- Gather a collection of books of poetry for children to browse whenever possible so that they realise where poems come from.
- Make suitable dictionaries easily available.
- Create a comfortable whole class seating arrangement so that every child can read the poster and participate fully in every aspect of the lesson.

Teachers and students need to do the following when conducting a poetry literacy hour:

1. Reading the prime text: Make this free of interruptions, unrushed and with a short pause at the end for the children to contemplate what they have heard. It should be a memorable moment in the day.
2. Choral speaking: Ensure that the children's first engagement with the prime text is enjoyable by developing their choral speaking of it briskly. They should already be familiar with the poem through attempting to learn it during the weekend so this should easily be possible. Try various combinations of voices, aiming to develop a good performance by the end of the week.
3. Points for discussion: Ensure that as many children as possible participate in the initial discussion of the poem by asking them – in small groups – to work out answers. Rather than waiting for hands to go up, target a group each time so that during the week every child will have to answer a question like this. Alternatively, the groups could each have a task card which targets a particular aspect of the poem's meaning. For instance, in e.e.cummings's 'in Just-' (Year 4 below) one of the tasks might be 'Find out what the boys have been playing', which will require them to find and interpret the lines 'and eddieandbill come/running from marbles and/piracies'. This should become a five-minute exercise in the first lesson.
4. Words and sentences: Identify the prime text's most important features and direct the first effort into them (e.g. the rhyme pattern in 'Storm' and the personification in 'The Birth of the Foal'). Follow this with other forms of analysis which serve both the overt literacy purposes and the children's understanding and experience of the poem.
5. Group and individual work: In most of the following examples group work tasks are set for three sets. However, to make the situation manageable each of the three sets will need to be divided in two, making six groups altogether. Each of these groups will require a helper. There will be the class teacher and, in most cases, a Nursery Nurse. The other four helpers might be students, parents, high school students on placement or older pupils.

Teachers need to make it very clear exactly what tasks the children are expected to do and how best to help them to do it. The teacher has to ensure that she works intensively with the groups twice each during the week. The Nursery Nurse should also see each group twice in the week.

A week's lessons for Reception

Prime text: 'Storm'[2]
> Wild winds
> call, call.
>
> Rain, hail
> fall, fall.
>
> Fresh gales
> squall, squall.
>
> Tossed trees
> tall, tall
>
> Crash down
> all, all.

Support text: 'It was Cat'[3]
> Cat crept in.
> Cat climbed up.
> Clatter went the dishes.
> Crash went the plates.
> Cat climbed down.
> Cat crept out.
> "Cracked are the dishes,
> you clumsy little boy!"

Secondary texts: (Appendix I):
Set One: 'The key to the kingdom'[4]
Set Two: 'Blessings'[5]
Set Three: 'Up here'[6]

Sharing the prime and support texts and working with the words (30 minutes)

1. Make flash cards for 'cr' and 'cl' and ask the children what sounds these letters make and to chant each sound very clearly when you point at it.
2. Write the sounds on the board and ask for examples of words containing them. Make lists of 'cr' and 'cl' words and get the children chanting them.
3. Pin up 'It was Cat' and read it to the class. Ask them to join in the next reading. Can they spot all the 'cr' and 'cl' words in the poem? As they say the words add them to the lists.
4. Divide the class into two mixed ability groups, one to say 'cr' words, the other to say 'cl' words when you are reading the poem. Try this a few times, then allocate lines with 'cr' in to one group and those with 'cl' to the other. This time they must read the poem.

5. Pin up 'Storm' and invite the children to speak it with you. Take the poster down and invite them to try again to see how well they know it.
6. Ask what is special about the sounds in the poem. Aim to establish the rhyme based on the sound 'all' and list these words under 'all' on the board.
7. Get the children chanting these words clearly and rhythmically.
8. Ask them if they notice anything else. They might notice the alliteration of 'w' in 'Wild winds' or of 't' in 'Tossed trees'. They might also see the rhyming of the 'ai' sound in 'Rain, hail' and another 'cr' sound in 'Crash'.

Group work

1. All children – with help – copy out the lists of words under 'cr', 'cl', and 'all'. Set One – and other sets if they can – make an 'alliteration' list of 't' words and a list of words with the 'ai' sound in the middle, starting with 'rain' and 'hail'.
2. All children make a poem on an aspect of the weather, using a simple format like 'Wild winds/call, call' but not necessarily trying to rhyme it. This will be more successful if the children make poems based on the weather being currently experienced. As most children will not be writing independently, ask them to whisper their lines to you or a helper then have them scribed.
3. With the required help, the six groups of children read the poems allocated to them so that they read it out loud in unison, with clarity and expression. The helpers invite the children to say what they think the poem is about; what they notice about it; if they like it and what they like.
4. Ask helpers to ensure that every child says something about the poem and that appropriate word features are identified and listed.

Features to look for in the secondary texts are as follows:

Set One: 'Blessings'

- Look for the words which rhyme: 'bride-hide', 'dream-stream', 'green-scream', 'snake-lake', 'frond-pond' and 'road-load'. Can the children provide other words for each list?
- List the words which begin with 'bl', 'br', 'cl', 'cr', 'gl' and 'gr'.
- What else can they bless and why?

Set Two: 'The key to the kingdom'

- How many times can the children find 'In that', 'in the', 'on the', 'there is'?
- List the words beginning with 'b', 'c', 'f', 'h', 'k', 'l', 'r', 's', 't' and 'y'.
- Compare the use of 'c' (soft 's' sound) with 'k'. List other words in which 'c' is soft and words in which 'c' sounds like 'k'.

Set Three: 'Up here'.

- Look for words in the poem which end in 'ay'. Can they think of others?
- Focus on words for senses: 'see', 'hear', 'feel', 'smell' and 'taste'. How can you 'feel' thunder or 'taste' May?
- Where might they be 'Up here'?

Reviewing/presenting

In the final sharing children may share any of the following: a choral reading of their secondary text; a brief account of what they think it means; or readings of individual poems. Start the sharing with a choral speaking of 'Storm' without scripts and put the individual poems in a book for the children to read.

Further work

In the other four poetry literacy hour lessons of this set focus on:

- the beginning letter-sounds of each word (w, c, r, h, f, fr, g, squ, t, tr, cr, d);
- the long and short vowel sounds (short – i in 'wind', e in 'fresh', a in 'crash', o in 'tossed'; long – i in 'wild', ai in 'rain', a in 'call', a in 'gales', ow in 'down'); and
- the final letter-sounds (-ld, -nds, -ll, -n, -l, -sh, -s, -ed).
- Get the children working hard on saying the difficult sounds 'squ-',' -nds', and '-ld' then the words they occur in, 'squall, squall', 'winds' and 'wild', ensuring that, as far as possible they will pronounce those words perfectly clearly.

Links in the arts

1. Movement and dance: In the P.E. lesson get the children to explore the movements of the cat creeping into the kitchen, the clatter of the plates, the creeping back out and the child being chastised. Provide opportunities for the children – in groups – to make little storm dances with movements for 'wild winds'; the falling of rain and hail; trees being 'tossed' and crashing down. When finished these dances should accompany the choral speaking of the words.
2. Music: Get the children composing sound sequences on untuned instruments to represent the cat's movements; the encounter between the child and the parent; and the storm. These little pieces should also accompany the dances and the choral speaking of the poems.
3. Art: In the art lesson ask the children to draw or paint pictures of the cat in the kitchen; the child and the parent; and aspects of the storm. They should also draw the words from the poems which go with their pictures.

A week's lessons for Year One (Term 2)

Prime text: 'I saw a peacock'[7]

I saw a peacock with a fiery tail.
I saw a blazing comet drop down hail.
I saw a cloud with ivy circled round.
I saw a sturdy oak creep on the ground.
I saw a little ant swallow a whale.
I saw a raging sea brim full of ale.
I saw a drinking glass sixteen feet deep.
I saw a well full of men's tears that weep.
I saw their eyes all in a flame of fire.

I saw a house as big as Moon and higher.
I saw the sun in the middle of night.
I saw the man that saw this wondrous sight

Secondary texts: (Appendix I):
Set One: 'What's in there?'[8]
Set Two: 'There I saw'[9]
Set Three: 'Ed's head'[10]

Sharing the prime text

1. Pin up the poster and ask the children to follow the words as you speak them. Divide them into twelve groups with a competent reader in each.
2. Allocate a line to each group and have each line written out separately on a card. Ask the children to practise their own line until they can say it well.
3. When they have mastered the decoding of their lines, ask the children to speak them in voices suited to the ideas in the lines. For instance, they might raise their voices and exclaim 'sixteen feet deep' or speak 'fiery tail' in a flickery way to represent flames.
4. They might also use suitable hand and body gestures (e.g. the flats of hands rising up their faces for 'brim full' or fingers placed in front of eyes then opened out quickly and blazingly for 'their eyes all in a flame of fire').
5. Children to perform the poem, pointing to each line as you go along. Practise this. If it works ask the children to exchange cards. Try to produce a fluent, expressive recitation with gestures by the end of the week.

Word work

1. Clearly establish what the subject of each sentence is: peacock, comet, cloud, oak tree, ant, sea, glass, well, eyes, house, sun and man. To consolidate these prepare a card for each word with a picture on it.
2. Establish what is marvellous or special about each thing and why this is strange. Ensure that, by the end of the word work in the second lesson, every child knows what the things are and what is marvellous about each of them.
3. Emphasise this by setting each line as a painting early in the week.
4. Concentrate initially on the rhymes: 'tail-hail', 'round-ground', whale-ale', 'deep-weep', 'fire-higher', and 'night-sight'. Establish the notion of rhyme for each child as 'words that sound the same' and go through the pairs chanting them. In each case divide the class in half, perhaps even boys and girls, so that one half chants the first example and the other half chants the second. The children will then experience the echoing effect which is the essence of rhyme.
5. The substantial focus, however, should be on the initial consonant clusters (bl-, dr-, cl-, st-, cr-, gr-, sw-, br-, fl-) and the end consonant clusters (-ck, -ng, -nd, -tle, -nt, -ll, -ss, -n's, -dle). The children should practise speaking these sounds, aiming for clarity and accuracy of pronunciation.

6. Over the week compile charts for these sounds with the sound written large at the top, followed by examples in the poem and in any other words that the children can add. Ask them to test each other for recognition of the sound that goes with the writing and with an example in the poem.
7. Emphasise the connection between the formation of letters and the sound they make.

Group work: writing

1. Children to write the rhyming pairs and the various consonant clusters with examples into word-books.
2. Establish that the poem is about fantastic sights and that these sights are of ordinary things made fantastic because of being put together with something else which is ordinary. Thus a peacock's tail is on fire or a 'house' the size of the moon. What fantastic sights can they imagine? Ask them to make other ordinary things become fantastic, such as: 'I saw a field . . . . .'; 'I saw a bird's nest . . . . .', 'I saw a plate of food . . . . .' What can the children do to make these fantastic?
3. When you have tried these, ask the children to make up their own.

Set One: 'What's in there?'

- Divide the class in half to represent questioner and responder so that the speaking of the poem sounds like a play. Give the children the opportunity to try speaking both parts and to develop the most effective voices.
- Help the children to work out exactly what the poem means. Tell them that 'there' in the poem is Burnie's Hill and that the poem starts in late summer so that the gold and the money are the ripe grains. Once they have grasped this, ask them to work out answers to the following questions:
  a) What has the mousie got?
  b) The word 'wood' is used twice. The first time it means a wood you can walk in. What does it mean the second time?
  c) What did the water do and what happened to it?
  d) What happens to the 'brown bull'?
  e) When the snow melts on Burnie's Hill what season might we be in?
  f) Which seasons have we passed through?
- Children to write the following in their word-books: 'sh-share', '-ou-mousie-housie', '-nt-burnt', 'qu-quenched', 'dr-drank', 'br-brown', 'dr-dressed', '-lt-melted'.

Set Two: 'There I saw'

- Tell the children that 'rill' is an old word for 'stream'.
- Divide the class in half, one speaking the lines beginning 'I went . . . .' and the others speaking the lines beginning 'There I saw . . . . .'
- Children to discuss what was seen in each place and to mime the actions of each one. They might record their discussions as follows: 'high hill-climbing goat', 'running rill-ragged sheep'. . . . . and imagine what else might have been seen in each place and add these to the list.

- Children to look for the pairs of rhymes in the poem: 'hill–rill', 'sea–tree', 'goat–boat' and 'sheep–asleep' and to write them in their word-books.
- Ask them to find and list the following consonant clusters: '-nt-went', '-ll-hill-rill', 'cl-climbing', 'sh-sheep', 'gr-green', 'tr-tree', '-sl-asleep', '-ng-climbing-tossing'.

Set Three: 'Ed's head'

- Children to take one of four parts: the narrator, Ed, his mother and Mr. The Mr part can be shared out as he has the most to say. Make sure the voices alternate; it will be more interesting that way.
- Ask them to work out how all these things get into 'Ed's head when he's in bed', trying to establish that he is dreaming and to discuss what things get into their heads when they are dreaming.
- Children to write the simpler rhyming groups in their word-books: 'Ed-bed', 'dogs-logs'; also these consonant clusters: 'th three', 'str-streams', 'dr-dreams'.

Reviewing/presenting

Label the reviewing/presenting part of the week 'What fantastic things did we see?' Feature recitations of the four poems and a selection of the children's poems. Give it the subtitle 'What rhymes and sounds did we learn?' with revision of those in the prime text and a sharing of some from the group work.

Links in the arts

The prime text offers rich possibilities for development in your art lesson. The children might draw and paint each line of the poem, either individually or as part of a whole class wall painting. They might also make drawings and paintings from the secondary texts they shared in group work. To emphasise the fantastic nature of the images they have been reading about they should mix vivid, bright colours and make bold lines on large sheets of paper.

A week's lessons for Year Two (Term 2)

Prime text: 'The Sea'[11]

> The sea is a hungry dog,
> Giant and grey.
> He rolls on the beach all day,
> With his clashing teeth and shaggy jaws
> Hour upon hour he gnaws
> The rumbling, tumbling stones,
> And 'Bones, bones, bones, bones!'
> The giant sea-dog moans,
> Licking his greasy paws.
>
> And when the night wind roars
> And the moon rocks in the stormy cloud,

He bounds to his feet and snuffs and sniffs,
Shaking his wet sides over the cliffs,
And howls and hollos long and loud.

But on quiet days in May and June,
When even the grasses on the dune
Play no more their reedy tune,
With his head between his paws
He lies on the sandy shores
So quiet, so quiet, he scarcely snores.

Secondary texts, (Appendix I)
Set One: 'The tide rises, the tide falls'[12]
Set Two: 'Wild Iron'[13]
Set Three: 'Until I saw the sea'[14]

Sharing the prime text

1. Pin up the poster of 'The Sea'. This poem is ideal for development as a choral speaking piece for various combinations of voices. It is particularly effective when variations of volume and speed are applied.
2. Develop a class choral version in which layers of sound build up, beginning with one slow voice saying the first line, joined by three or four others for 'Giant and grey' and more and more for each line. Crescendo on 'Bones, bones, bones, bones!' with the whole class saying 'bones' the fourth time. The final two lines fall off, so have them spoken by the original five or six voices saying, 'The giant sea-dog moans' and the single voice saying 'Licking his greasy paws.'
3. Allocate parts in the opening 15 minutes of the first lesson. Practise at the start of subsequent lessons.

Word work

1. The most significant feature of the poem is the metaphor of the sea being a dog. Establish that a 'metaphor' is a sort of magic trick in which one thing is made into something else because it has some similarities. So 'The sea *is* a hungry dog'. It is not merely *like* 'a hungry dog'.
2. Ask the children to find examples of ways in which the sea *is* a dog and write some of them on the board.
3. Another important feature is the irregular rhyme scheme. Ask the children if they notice any rhymes in the poem and to give examples. Write a list and get the children to notice that whereas the 'aws' rhyme has seven examples, most others have only two or three examples. Point out that the same rhymes don't come every other line, but that they are mixed up across the poem.
4. Establish that some rhymes such as 'rumbling-tumbling' occur within one line.
5. Ask the children what they notice about the spellings of the rhyming words. Do they

notice that some rhymes have the same spelling of the rhyming sound: 'sniffs–cliffs' and 'June–dune–tune' but that others have different spellings: 'grey–day' and 'bones–moans'.

Group work

1. All children to write the aspects of the sea-dog metaphor in a line chart as follows: sea = dog-rolls-clashing teeth-shaggy jaws-gnaws stones and bones.
2. All children to write the lists of rhymes and add their own words to the list, looking for words with the same and with different kinds of spelling. They should check these words in their dictionaries.
3. Set One and, perhaps, Set Two briefly to write about 'The Sea' and their favourite parts in it.
4. With the required help, the six groups (from three sets) speak the poems allocated to them in unison, with clarity and expression. They divide their poems into parts. Helpers then invite the children to say what their poem is about, what they notice and whether they like it or not.
5. Children to write poems which are suggested by the secondary texts as suggested in the ideas for sets below.

Set One: 'The tide rises, the tide falls'

- Children to find the best way to speak the poem themselves. However, suggest that the chorus 'The tide rises, the tide falls' be spoken by some members of the group as a background to the speaking of the rest of the poem.
- Children to find and list meanings of difficult or old words: 'twilight', 'hastens', 'efface', 'steeds', 'stalls' and 'hostler'. Teacher to prepare a glossary.
- Children to look for and list the rhymes and work out their pattern: 'falls-calls-brown-town-falls', a-a-b-b-a.
- Children to count the number of times each rhyme occurs and check how the rhyming sounds are spelt. Are they the same or different? Make notes.
- Each child to find an answer to one or two of the following questions: 'What does the tide do? – the curlew do? – the twilight do? – the traveller do? – the darkness? the sea? the little waves? – the morning? – the steeds? – the hostler? – the day?' 'What does the traveller *not* do?' These should be found very quickly (2 mins).
- Writing: ask the children to imagine the traveller coming to the town in a hurry, staying overnight and leaving. Remind them of the atmosphere in the poem. Try to induce that quiet, mysterious feeling. Say that perhaps there are some verses of the poem missing, the ones that might have been written about what happened in the town and what happens to the traveller next. Avoid story prose by asking them to write a line which describes the place the traveller is in next and add a line about what happens. Aim to get two five-line verses from each child.

Set Two: 'Wild Iron'

- After they have worked on speaking the poem with emphasis on its rhythmic qualities, tell the children that 'foundering' means that the 'gale' is so harsh that it makes ships sink. To founder means to sink. Children to write this.

- Ask them what they notice about the poem, trying to establish that ideas are repeated as in 'Sea go dark, go dark with wind'. Children to find and write another example of this repetition.
- Teach the children also that some words in the poem sound like the thing they are describing. For instance, 'swinging' and 'clanging' sound like corrugated iron on an old shed in the wind.
- Children to find the answer to one of these questions: 'What does the sea go? – feet? – thoughts?', 'What does the iron do? – the gale?' This to be done quickly (3 mins). They write them.
- Writing: children to think back to the last time they experienced bad weather. They write what the bad weather was. Ask them to imagine themselves in that bad weather and to write one line about it. Ask them to add new lines, line by line about being in bad weather.

Set Three: 'Until I saw the sea'

- This is a quiet, contemplative poem so single voices will carry it better than groups. Children, therefore, should read it two lines each at a time as in:
  1st child: Until I saw the sea/I did not know . . . . .
  2nd child: . . . . . that wind/could wrinkle water so.
- Children to try different lines each to gain familiarity with the whole.
- After they have spoken the words sufficiently, focus the children's attention on the three key words, 'wrinkle', 'splinter' and 'breathes'.
- Establish the meanings of these words through questioning, then involve them in discussing how wind might 'wrinkle water'; how sun might 'splinter' the blue of the sea; and how the sea might appear to breathe on the shore.
- Demonstrate with a pan of water, a light source and by creating the effect of water lapping over a mass.
- Children to look at the rhyming words in the poem: 'know-so', 'knew-blue' and 'before-shore'. What do they notice about these rhymes? Establish that in two of them the sounds are spelt differently. Children to make lists and add examples.
- Turn to the interesting beginning letter sounds – 'kn', 'wr', 'spl' and 'wh'; final letter sounds – 'kle', 'ter' and 'thes'; and middle vowel sounds – 'o' in 'not' compared with 'o' in 'whole' and 'o' in 'shore', 'ou' in 'could' compared with 'ou' in out', 'ea' in 'sea' and 'breathes'. Children to list the sounds and the words they are in and practise saying each sound followed by the words.
- Writing: children to experiment with water: pouring it from different heights onto different surfaces; watching it coming from the tap and going down the plughole; squirting and swishing it. Each time they should find suitable words to describe what they see, hear and feel, as Lilian Moore does with her ideas in 'wrinkle', 'splinter' and 'breathe'. Children to create their own ideas from observing the water and to use them in their own poems.

Reviewing/presenting

Start the session with a choral recitation of 'The Sea'. Then spend the sharing session on the work which has come from the secondary texts. Members of each group to speak their secondary text poem; some to provide brief accounts of these poems; others to read their own poems.

Links in the arts

1. Music: 'The Sea' describes – quite precisely – a set of sounds which can provide opportunities for children to make a tone poem or film-type score in a music lesson: using percussion and other musical instruments, children to find ways of making the basic sounds depicted in the three verses. Verses to be called 'movements' in the music lesson with the tempo listed for each one as follows:
   — 1st Movement (*moderato*): quite a loud movement, neither fast nor slow. Children to use the following key words and phrases for ideas: 'clashing teeth', 'gnaws/The rumbling, tumbling stones', 'bones', 'moans' and 'Licking'. Untuned percussion instruments to be used.
   — 2nd Movement (*allegro*): a lively movement, varying from loud to quiet (from 'roars' to 'sniffs' to 'howls'). The key words and phrases here are: 'roars', 'stormy', 'snuffs and sniffs', 'Shaking', 'howls and hollos loud and long'. Use a range of wind instruments, strings and voices.
   — 3rd Movement (*andante*): quiet and moderately slow. The key words are 'quiet', 'grasses', 'dunc', 'paws', 'lies' and 'scarcely snores'.
2. Dance: Children to explore the various moods of the sea and the wind, attempting to make shapes and movements which are both sealike and doglike: quick scampering wave movements, slow lazy lapping movements. These to be tried individually, in pairs, large groups and whole class. Picking up ideas from the Set Three poem, the children in large groups attempt to make wrinkle shapes, splintering movements and the lapping, ripples made by wind on water. If this works, the children to make a dance, containing the basic *motifs* and performed to the tone poem made in the music lesson.
3. Art: Children to make semi-abstract drawings which suggest both the sea and the dog in any of their moods. If the initial drawings work, develop into paintings.

A week's lessons for Year Three (Term 3)

Prime text: 'Little Trotty Wagtail'[15]

> Little trotty wagtail, he went in the rain,
> And tittering, tottering sideways he ne'er got straight again.
> He stooped to get a worm and look'd up to get a fly,
> And then he flew away e'er his feathers they were dry.
>
> Little trotty wagtail, he waddled in the mud,
> And left his little footmarks, trample where he would.
> He waddled in the water-pudge, and waggle went his tail,
> And he chirrup up his wings to dry upon the garden rail.

Little trotty wagtail, you nimble all about,
And in the dimpling water-pudge you waddle in and out;
Your home is nigh at hand, and in the warm pigsty,
So, little master wagtail, I'll bid you a goodbye.

Secondary texts: (Appendix I):
Set One: 'The Pelican Chorus' (extract)[16]
Set Two: 'The Owl'[17]
Set Three: 'Ducks' Ditty'[18]

Sharing the prime text

1. In their choral speaking of this poem the children should try to capture the regular, jaunty rhythm, meant by Clare to represent the movements of this dainty bird. It is a quiet poem in praise of a well-loved creature and, therefore, requires individual or small groups of voices.

2. The children will need to enunciate individual word sounds very clearly as the poem demands fairly quick speaking. For instance, in the first line it is essential that the double-t sounds are clearly spoken. The children must avoid the glottal stop. This mispronunciation, which some of us do, substitutes for the sound of the -t-, which is made by the teeth, a sound at the back of the throat. In the poem the double-t sounds are essential as they represent the pattering sounds of the bird's feet. So, 'Little' is 'litl' and not 'li-ul'.

3. There is a tendency with this poem for children to speak it in sing-song, monotonous voices with too much stress on rhymes. To avoid this, ask them always to have the bird in mind, its rapid footsteps and its constant wagging movements. By concentrating their efforts on pronouncing the consonants precisely within a rhythmic way of speaking the children should avoid this.

4. Another key factor for the children's work with this poem is the early identification of the bird itself. 'Little trotty wagtail' is the Pied Wagtail, which is common even in towns and cities these days. It is frequently found in school playgrounds, particularly after breaks when it comes to eat dropped crumbs!

5. The children's understanding of the poem will be greatly enhanced if they are able actually to see a Pied Wagtail and, if it is in the school grounds, to call it 'Trotty'!

6. Writing: ask the children to name their favourite birds for writing poems about. It is better if the birds chosen are ones the children have actually seen rather than ones chosen from a book. Once the children have made their choices ask them to write the bird's name then close eyes and imagine it. What is the first picture they have? They write that as vividly as they can and not like they are writing it for a bird identification book. They must try to 'capture the spirit of the bird' or – in Ted Hughes' phrase – 'turn the bird into words'. They close eyes and imagine it again. What else do they see or hear? For instance, where is the bird? Is it singing? Is it feeding, flying or on its eggs? They write their next imagination about the bird and continue doing this until they can think of no more to write. Alternatively, the

children might observe a bird from the classroom and find vivid ways of writing what they see to try to 'turn it into words'.

Word and sentence work

1. Ask the children what they notice about the sounds at the ends of lines. Establish that they rhyme in couples or couplets: 'rain–again', 'fly–dry', 'mud–would', 'tail–rail', 'about–out' and 'pigsty–goodbye'. Draw the children's attention to the irregular spellings in 'mud–would' and 'pigsty–goodbye' and ask for other examples of this. List on blackboard and in word-books.
2. Talk about the archaisms: 'ne'er' (never), 'ere' (before) and 'nigh' (near). Point out that 'ne'er' is written like that so that the rhythm of the poem is kept regular. 'Never' would add a syllable to their lines. Add that 'look'd' and 'chirrupt' are older ways of writing 'looked' and 'chirruped'. List these.
3. Next, focus on the words Clare uses to describe the bird's movements: 'trotty', 'tittering', 'tottering', 'went', 'stooped', 'look'd up', 'flew away', 'waddled', 'trample', 'waggle', 'chirrup' and 'nimble'. Separate them into words which vividly describe the way he moves ('tittering', 'stooped') and those which merely indicate movement ('went', 'flew away'). These movements will be consolidated very well by working on them in movement lessons. List these.
4. Talk about the references to the bird walking in the wetness: 'rain', 'mud', 'footmarks', 'water-pudge', and 'dimpling water-pudge'. What do the children see? Draw out the differences between the simple 'mud' to the more poetic idea of 'dimpling water-pudge'. Spend time on this differentiation and list the examples.

Group work

Some of the group work time should be set aside for the children to continue writing their bird poems and for re-drafting them.

Set One: 'The Pelican Chorus'

- The children to spend sufficient time getting the rhythm of this poem right in their choral speaking of it. It will help if they are allowed actually to work out a dance to go with the chorus.
- This work to lead to consideration of the rhyme scheme, which is similar to that in 'Little trotty wagtail'. Children to list the pairs of rhymes in their word-books.
- They should also consider the alliteration, which accentuates the rhythm in certain lines. For instance in 'And when the sun, sinks slowly down' the -s- sounds actually slow the rhythm down to match the idea of the sun's slow decline. The children should look for all the examples of alliteration and, if time allows, describe the effect it has on the poem's rhythm. They might also make up some more alliterating names for pelicans using the 'Pl-' prefix.
- Next they should discuss the pictures which Lear creates in the poem, particularly vividly in the second verse. Each of them to make pencil sketches of two of them.

Which are the key adjectives which help them to see these pictures? For instance, they might draw the 'islands' and work out that it is the words 'long, 'bare' and 'brown' which provide the clues. This will make the children realise the value of adjectives to a poem. Children to list the adjectives.

Set Two: 'The Owl'

- Explain to the children that this poem was written when windmills and watermills ground corn into flour, when milkmaids milked the cows by hand and took the milk into the dairy which was part of the farm. This was a long time ago and those days there were lots of 'white owls'.
- The children should find out which species of owl Tennyson means. Is it a Tawny Owl, a Little Owl or a Barn Owl? Make books available for them to decide.
- Provide the children with a glossary of the following words: 'wits' – senses (hearing, seeing, smelling, tasting, touching); 'belfry' – church tower; 'latch' – door fastener, which you lift; 'hath' – has; 'thatch' – roof made of reeds; 'thrice' – three times; 'roundelay' – short song.
- For their speaking of the poem, children to use paired voices, specialising in one rhyme each at a time. So, for instance, the first pair will speak the first and third lines of a verse, the second pair the second and fourth and the third pair the last two lines. For special effect all the children to join in the repeated lines, 'And the whirring sail goes round' and 'Twice or thrice his roundelay'.
- Children to discuss what time of day is being described. When they have decided this they should identify the lines in the poem which are the clues. Each of them to make a quick sketch of one thing which proves what time of day it is.
- Paying special attention to the words in italics, they should discuss the meaning of the following: 'the far-off stream is *dumb*', '*whirring* sail goes round', '*warming* his five wits', *merry* milkmaids click the latch', '*rarely* smells the new-mown hay' and 'Twice or thrice his roundelay'.
- After investigating the poem, children should be encouraged to mime some of it: 'cats run home', 'whirring sail', 'white owl in the belfry', 'merry milkmaids click the latch', and 'cock hath sung'. This physical work will consolidate meanings, bring added enjoyment and make the poem more memorable.

Set Three: 'Ducks' Ditty'

- This highly rhythmic poem requires a fairly quick and lively performance with plenty of stress on the last line of each verse, particularly the first words: 'Up', 'Busy', 'Cool', 'Dabbling' and 'Up'. If possible, the children to have the opportunity of working out a dance to accompany their reading.
- Establish that this poem is from *The Wind in the Willows* and describes the ducks in part of the river. The children to discuss exactly what the ducks are doing – feeding in the river by putting their heads in the water, tails up and reaching down for weeds. They should list the names of the places where the ducks go to do this: 'backwater', 'rushes' and 'undergrowth'. Other words and meanings to be established

are: 'bills' (beaks), 'roach' (species of fish), 'larder' (food storage place) and 'Swifts' (birds). Where are the swifts and where are the ducks?

- The children should try to see the precise picture 'painted' in each verse. What exactly do they see? Each verse to be drawn by members of the set. A particularly interesting one is the second verse and its 'Yellow feet a-quiver,/Yellow bills all out of sight'.
- For words work the rhymes should be listed first: 'tall–all', 'quiver–river', 'swim–dim', 'be–free' and 'call–all'. Other learning points of this kind are: 'backwater' is made from 'back' and 'water', and 'undergrowth' from 'under' and 'growth'; double-b in 'dabbling' – look for other examples of double-b words.

Reviewing/presenting

The end of the week presentation will be greatly enhanced by performances of the movements described in the poems. There will also be drawings and paintings to show as well as choral readings and presentations of meanings.

Links in the arts

1. Art: Each set's group work recommends that the children make drawings to develop understanding of the ideas in the poems. These drawings could make successful first draft (sketchbook) material for paintings in the art lesson.
2. Dance and movement: As already stated several times in this section, the prime text and the secondary texts actually require movement work in the P.E. lesson to illuminate their subject matter and their rhythms. The lessons should begin with shared work on 'Little trotty wagtail' based on the verbs. This work can successfully be developed as warm up activities for individuals and the group work as compositions in dance: the pelican dance, the dance in Tennyson's 'The Owl', and the ducks' dance.
3. Music: The rhythm in 'Little trotty wagtail' will be consolidated very strongly if the children clap it, tap it and, perhaps, make simple tunes for it on the glockenspiel, xylophone, chime bars or keyboards. If these compositions prove successful they can be used to enhance the movement work. The pelican and ducks' dances would benefit from composition work of this kind.

A week's lessons for Year Four (Term 3)

Prime text: 'in Just-'[19]
    in Just-
    spring   when the world is mud-
    luscious the little
    lame balloonman

    whistles   far   and wee

and eddieandbill come
running from marbles and
piracies and it's
spring

when the world is puddle-wonderful

the queer
old balloonman whistles
far   and   wee
and bettyand isbel come dancing

from hop-scotch and jump-rope and

it's spring
and
    the

        goat-footed

balloonMan   whistles
far
and
wee

Secondary texts: (Appendix I)
Set One: 'Meg Merrilies'[20]
Set Two: 'Old Man'[21]
Set Three: 'The Ugly Child'[22]

Sharing texts

1. Pin up the poster of 'in Just-'. Although this poem has its lively, joyful moments it is essentially a quiet poem. It should, therefore, be spoken solo and by small groups of voices. The references to the 'balloonman' particularly demand the single voice speaking. The references to the two groups of children would best be spoken as duets of boys – 'eddieandbill' and girls – 'bettyand isbel'.
2. A good way of making a start, however, is simply to go round the class allowing each child one line to say, even if that line is only 'far'. It will introduce the sound of the poem to them well.
3. Discuss the punctuation here only as it influences the way the poem should be spoken. A good rule of thumb is to recognise the extra spaces, as seen in 'whistles far   and   wee' by pausing for longer, and to acknowledge the newly coined words, as in 'Just-' and 'balloonman' by making each of them sound like one word. Doing this will be fun for the children and lead naturally into the word and sentence study section.

4. Ask the children to tell you exactly what they see when they 'imagine' this poem, to describe the balloonman, the boys and the girls, to say where it is all happening. What are the three ways in which the balloonman is introduced? How do they feel about him? Is this a happy poem? Or a sad poem? Or something else?

Word and sentence work

1. Start by looking at the delicious coinings e.e.cummings has made: 'mud-luscious' and 'puddle-wonderful'. What do they notice? Teach them that there is internal rhyming in both coinings based on an 'uh' sound, so there is a sense in which they belong together.
2. What do these coinings make the children feel? What do they think e.e.cummings feels about mud and puddles? Dwell on this crucial language of the poem a little.
3. Draw the children's attentions to the following repeated phrases, which also connect with the joyful feeling in those two coinings: 'when the world' and 'whistles far and wee'. What do they notice about the sound of these phrases?
4. Establish the alliteration of the 'w' sound which gives these phrases a light, almost flying off sound like balloons! Make sure the children know exactly what alliteration is and consolidate this by pointing to its use with the 'l' sound in 'mud-luscious the little lame balloonman' which makes the listener pause to think about that character.
5. Many children, who by now should be using a range of punctuation marks, will see that e.e.cummings does not use it properly! This should provide both teacher and children with some enjoyment.
6. Get the children to say where the punctuation would come if written by someone else, but under no circumstances set a worksheet task in which the poem is corrected!
7. After you have gone through this on the poster, ask the children if they like the poem as it is or if they would prefer it with 'correct' punctuation. Tell them, though, that e.e.cummings could get away with it but that they cannot!

Group work

1. All children to write the two new coinings for spring, 'mud-luscious' and 'puddle-wonderful', then add one of their own to this list by putting two words together.
2. They then focus for their own writing on whatever season they are experiencing. With his lame leg, yet his balloons and his whistling, the balloonman embodies the spirit of spring coming. So do eddieandbill and bettyandisbel with their games. Can the children think of a character or characters who might be just right for summer, autumn or winter? If so, they could put them in their poems.
3. Ask the children to look out of the window and think of things they can write about the season they are in. Their poems might begin 'In spring when', 'In summer when', 'In autumn when' or 'In winter when', then introduce just a small number of well described features of the season, including the characters if they can think of any.

Set One: 'Meg Merrilies'

Explain to the children that this poem was written more than 170 years ago and that some spellings and actual words have changed since then. Provide them with the following glossary: 'Gipsy' – traveller, originally coming from an area near modern day Romania; 'liv'd' – lived (explain that poets often left letters out like this in those days); 'heath' – quite high up land where heather grows; 'turf'- sods of grass; 'swart' – dark-coloured; 'broom' – heathland bush with yellow flowers and seeds in pods; 'o' – of; 'craggy' – rocky; 'larchen' – larch; ''stead' – instead; 'woodbine' – a pretty flower; 'garlanding' – wreath or crown made of flowers; 'glen' – valley; 'yew' – evergreen tree; 'Cottagers' – poor people who lived in small country houses; 'Margaret Queen' – a queen of England in the middle ages; 'Amazon' – one of a tribe of women of the Amazon in South America, noted for their strength and height; 'agone' – ago.

- The poem is a kind of ballad, which carries a simple story. It is, therefore, best spoken by single voices, taking turns a verse at a time. Suggest to the children that they speak the words as if they are telling a story and to try to be expressive. They must avoid a montononous tone to their voices.

- When they have worked on this several times, they should work out together what the story is.

- A key aspect to the poem's meaning is the comparison between what Meg has and what wealthy people have. Thus, for a bed she has the grass out of doors, for wine she has dew. The children to compile a list of things that Meg has and what the items represent in a wealthy person's life, like this: 'sods of grass for a bed', 'out of doors for a house', 'blackberries for her fruit', 'pods of broom for currants' and so on.

- Children to work out how Meg occupied herself. What did she do with her time? Children to write a list of these jobs.

- They should discuss Meg's character. What sort of person was Meg? This to be done with lists of opposites: 'Was she good or bad?', 'Was she rich or poor?', 'Was she lazy or hard-working?', 'Was she cowardly or brave?' The children to describe her and draw her.

- For words work the children to begin by investigating and listing the rhyming words: 'Moors – doors', 'broom – tomb', and so on. What do they notice about the spellings of some of these sounds? In many cases the same sounds are made with different spellings. Children to underline these differences and find other examples of them.

- For sentence and verse study the children firstly to compare the last verse with the others. The last one sort of summarises Meg's character and springs the surprise that she is long dead. So it has six lines instead of four. They should also look at the punctuation. They might notice, for instance, that each verse – except the last – is one sentence. The verses contain single continuous ideas or themes with examples. Children to choose one verse each and (a) write what the idea or theme is; and (b) list the examples of this idea. For instance, the third verse is about Meg's family and the examples are brothers and sisters ('craggy hills' and 'larchen trees').

Set Two: 'Old Man'

- This is another poem to be spoken by single voices. Start by asking the children to read round a line each at a time, trying to put expression into their voices without overdoing it. For instance, 'cold and bitter' might be spoken by a child who sounds as if shivering a little and 'hurries head down' might be spoken more quickly than the rest of that part of the poem.

- To begin their discussion the group needs to establish what is happening. The poet sees the man coming away from the corner shop. What next? Without using the descriptive words, the children to say precisely what the man is doing and where he is going. Why does he behave like he does? Then they should work out why this is different from normal. The word 'chatty' provides the clue.

- The most important feature of the poem is found in the use of fire imagery to describe the old man. Tell the children that the poet has deliberately used words associated with lighting fires in the grate at home when describing the old man. They should look for them and list them. They are as follows: 'his breath pours out like smoke', 'His eyes are sparks', 'his tight lips/put out his words' and 'scuttles'.

- The children to look for words which rhyme or which partly rhyme. Rhymes: 'Thickly–quickly', 'cold–old', 'Grimly–thinly', 'holds–coal–cold–cold'. This last one, which is the last part of the poem, is interesting in that it emphasises the idea of the coldness. Part rhymes: 'bitter–chatty–little–scuttles'. These part rhymes are interesting being based on double-t in the middle of certain words. Children to decide what effect this has. Guide them to realise that it has the effect of teeth chattering with the cold and provide a good example of 'onomatopoeia' or words that sound like the thing they are describing. Children to list these and write what the effect of them is.

- They should then look for examples of alliteration: 'hurries–head down', 'smoke–sparks–stares–straight', 'coal–cold–cold'. Children to discuss the effect of this on the poem, which is to speed up the rhythm and underline the fact that the old man is in a hurry.

Set Three: 'The Ugly Child'

- Discussion should focus initially on how the children see themselves. Do they think they are 'ugly', 'good-looking', 'nice' or 'horrible'? Ask them why they think the child in the poem thinks he or she is ugly? Establish that one reason might be that he/she has been told it.

- Focus on how they see other people. Are there people who they think are ugly or beautiful, avoiding naming names? Do they call people names and make them feel that they are no good? Does the child in the poem deserve to feel he/she is ugly simply for the reasons listed? Ask the children to make lists of these reasons starting with the word 'uninteresting'.

- Draw the children's attention to the rhyme scheme, a very simple one – every other line ends in a rhyme. Ask the children to list them: 'true–view', 'sad–bad', 'nose–hose' and 'be–me' and direct them to notice that in one pair of rhymes the rhyming sound is spelt differently. Can they think of other words with that 'oo' sound, which are spelt differently again ('chew', 'do', 'queue', 'too'). Ask them to list these words also.

- Other important spellings to look at and list are as follows: verb tense changes which add 'd' ('hear–heard', 'hope–hoped') compared to those that add 'ed' (look–looked');

polysyllabic words ('certainly', 'uninteresting', 'Imagine' and 'because'); and words with double consonants in the middle ('mirror', 'better' and 'skinny').

Reviewing/presenting

Begin the end of week session with a recitation of cummings' 'in Just-' and of the three secondary texts: 'Meg Merrilies' by John Keats, 'Old Man' by Dennis Carter, and 'The Ugly Child' by Elizabeth Jennings. Members of each set should then say, from a prepared text, what the set's poem was about, what they think of it and why, and highlight any parts of particular interest. Some children should then read their own poems.

Links in the arts

- Drama and dance: Take a lesson in which the children work on the movements of the balloonman, including the sense of the balloons floating on the ends of strings. They should move as if they are weightless themselves as a contrast with the balloonman's awkward movements. Stress this contrast. A further contrast is in the movements of the boys and the girls coming from their games. Perhaps they move lightly and quickly or maybe clumsily surge in. This needs to be discussed with the class. Divide the class into mixed ability groups of five and ask the groups to make a dance in which the boys and girls play their games then, when they see him, they go to the balloonman and buy balloons from him, finally going off to play with the balloons. Develop the group work further into spoken drama with the two sets of children playing their games – this time with speech and maybe chants – then coming to the balloonman and talking with him.
- Music: Ask the children in their groups to make a short sound sequence for the poem which can accompany their dance and drama. They should use light percussion instruments, chime bars, glockenspiels and xylophones. When they have done this they should make a graphic score so that another group can play it while they do the dance/drama.
- Art: Get the children exploring in paint the possibilities in the 'mud-luscious', 'puddle-wonderful' world of early spring. Ask a group to work on a full-size portrait of the balloonman with his balloons. Set the children individual portraits of the boys playing their games (in pirate costumes?) and the girls playing hopscotch or jump-rope.

A week's lessons for Year Five (Term 2)

Although the Year Five poem, 'Kubla Khan' by Samuel Taylor Coleridge, is both long and complex it is suitable for this age group and has been taught successfully on several occasions in my experience. For instance, successful dance and art work was carried out in Taliesin Junior School in the 1980s and it was included in a pilot project during the pilot stage of Clwyd Poetry Project's work.[23] However, in order to make best use of the poem to develop children's literacy, there are certain changes to the approach so far adopted in these literacy lessons and minor infringements of the NLS 'Framework for teaching'. These differences are as follows:

● Children attempt a reading of it with their parents but only learn particular lines of it, prior to the literacy lessons.
● No secondary texts are set, but the groups focus on extracts of 'Kubla Khan' itself and these groups are of mixed ability rather than being sets.
● Links in the arts considered as essential to a full engagement with the poem.

Prime text: 'Kubla Khan'[24] (The rules are to indicate manageable portions of the text for children to learn.)

> In Xanadu did Khubla Khan
> A stately pleasure-dome decree:
> Where Alph, the sacred river, ran
> Through caverns measureless to man
> Down to a sunless sea.
> So twice five miles of fertile ground
> With walls and towers were girdled round:
> And there were gardens bright with sinuous rills,
> Where blossomed many an incense-bearing tree;
> And here were forests ancient as the hills,
> Enfolding sunny spots of greenery.
>
> ---
>
> But oh! that deep romantic cavern which slanted
> Down the green hill athwart a cedarn cover!
> A savage place! as holy and enchanted
> As e'er beneath a waning moon was haunted
> By woman wailing for her demon lover!
> And from this cavern, with ceaseless turmoil seething,
> As if this earth in fast, thick pants were breathing,
> A mighty fountain momently was forced:
> Amid whose swift half-intermitted burst
> Huge fragments vaulted like rebounding hail,
> Or chaffy grain beneath the thresher's flail:
> And 'mid these dancing rocks at once and ever
> It flung up momently the sacred river.
>
> ---
>
> Five miles meandering with a mazy motion
> Through wood and dale the sacred river ran,
> Then reached the caverns measureless to man,
> And sank in tumult to a lifeless ocean:
> And 'mid this tumult Kubla heard from far
> Ancestral voices prophesying war!
>
> The shadow of the dome of pleasure
> Floated midway on the waves;
> Where was heard the mingled measure

From the fountain and the caves.
It was a miracle of rare device,
A sunny pleasure-dome with caves of ice!

A damsel with a dulcimer
In a vision once I saw:
It was an Abyssinian maid,
And on her dulcimer she played,
Singing of Mount Arbora.
Could I revive within me
Her symphony and song,
To such a deep delight 'twould win me,
That with music loud and long,
I would build a dome in air.
That sunny dome! those caves of ice!
And all who heard should see them there,
And all should cry, Beware! Beware!
His flashing eyes, his floating hair!
Weave a circle round him thrice,
And close your eyes with holy dread,
For he on honey-dew hath fed,
And drunk the milk of Paradise.

Sharing the prime text

1. Divide the class into eight groups. Two groups of children to learn each part of the text. It is important, however, that they have some familiarity with the whole poem as quickly as possible.
2. More than in any other poem it is essential that the teacher prepare herself by reading the poem out loud several times to get it right and come to the first lesson with a point of view about the poem and what it is about. A glossary will be necessary – see below – but many of the unknown words could be found in a dictionary.
3. The children then to follow the poem in their own copies as you read it out loud to them. After this first reading point out the glossary and talk about the most important words on it: the imaginary names and the 'pleasure-dome'.
4. The groups then read the poem out loud in their parts at least twice.
5. Establish at this point that the poem's subtitle is 'A vision in a dream' and that the poem is a product of Coleridge's pure imagination. Talk about the nature of dreams in which the dreamer's mind jumps from one happening or image to another, which seems unconnected. Summarise that this is a narrative poem, but that the story is a dream story rather than a real one.

Word and sentence work

1. Make a large poster version of this glossary:
   Xanadu: an imaginary country;

Kubla Khan: an imaginary ruler;

pleasure-dome: a place for all kinds of enjoyment under a domed roof;

Alph: an imaginary river;

girdled round: surrounded as if by tight-fitting clothing;

sinuous rills: thin, twisty streams;

incense-bearing tree: tree which contains the resin which makes frankincense;

cedarn: containing cedar trees;

e'er: ever;

demon lover: passionate, frightening lover?

chaffy grain: the skins on grains of wheat;

thresher's flail: a tool used for beating the chaff of grains off wheat;

meandering: wandering here and there;

ancestral voices: voices from past members of their people;

of rare device: of great craftsmanship;

dulcimer: an ancient stringed instrument which is played by striking the strings;

Mount Arbora: an imaginary mountain;

symphony: piece of music;

'twould: it would;

honey-dew: ideally sweet substance.

2. The children to copy the explanations of the words which are in their extracts for learning.
3. Children in their groups to investigate the pattern of their rhymes under the supervision of the teacher. The pattern is more complex than in many narrative poems: a-b-a-a-b-c-c-d-e-d-e in the first part (to 'spots of greenery').
4. This complex pattern continues throughout the poem. Groups to be asked to work out reasons for it. Is it to represent the meandering nature of the dream narratives?

Group work

Words and sentences

1. Ask the children to recognise and list – in pairs – the key nouns with their adjectives and the key verbs with their adverbs in their parts of the text. The question to determine which are key should be "Which nouns (excluding proper nouns) and adjectives (verbs and adverbs) do you see most clearly as you hear or speak the poem?"
2. Thus, in the first part the answer for nouns and adjectives might be: 'stately pleasure-dome', 'sacred river', 'caverns measureless', 'sunless sea', 'fertile ground', 'sinuous rills', 'incense-bearing tree' and 'forests ancient'.
3. As they do this it will become clear to the children that almost every noun is defined more clearly with an adjective.
4. An analysis of this kind for verbs and adverbs will reveal less consistency. For instance, the first part has virtually no adverbs to modify its verbs, whereas in the section beginning 'But oh! that deep romantic chasm' carries quite complex adverbs

and adverbial clauses. The 'earth' for instance, is 'breathing' in 'fast, thick pants', the fountain 'flung up momently' and the river 'sank in tumult'.

5. This indicates a considerable difference between the two parts of the poem, the former being relatively simple and descriptive, the latter being complex and detailed. The children will infer some of this difference by carrying out this analysis.

Writing

1. Ask the children to choose from the following list of items and add their own lines to the 'Kubla Khan' vision: Kubla Khan, the Demon Lover or the Abyssinian maid. Ask them then to imagine their character, closing their eyes and picturing that character. Children to write what they see in a vivid, dreamlike way, as in the poem itself.
2. Ask them to imagine they see the pleasure-dome in the distance. Say to them, "Write a verse about it. Go towards it and when you are near it, write a verse about that. Find the way in. Another verse. Inside. A final verse."
3. Ask the children to imagine they are walking in the gardens of Xanadu. They hear voices. Say, "Hide behind a hedge and watch. What do you see? Describe it vividly."
4. Ask them to close eyes and imagine the 'caverns measureless to man'. What do they hear, feel and see? Write these as a poem.

Discussion

In their small groups the children finally to work out what they think their part of the poem means and a member of each group should report this to the whole class in the longer plenary session on the last day.

Reviewing/presenting

Time needs to be found to make the presenting/reviewing part of this poetry/literacy work to include the children's responses in the arts. If possible some kind of concert, perhaps at the end of the half term, should be organised. This will facilitate a more analytical review during the actual literacy week.

Links in the arts

1. Art: The poem is a treasure-trove of visual material and there are hundreds of potential subjects for drawing, painting, sculpting, construction work, fabric work and printing. Rather than setting subjects for the children, it is better to revisit their own special part of the poem. Ask them to choose a phrase or line that appeals strongly to their imaginations and work out how to develop it. For instance, a child might choose a passage which is clearly narrative and pictorial such as 'A savage place! . . . . .' to 'demon lover!' which might depict something like a passionate woman, mouth open beneath a half moon. On the other hand, the following two lines about the 'chasm, with ceaseless turmoil seething' would invite a more abstract expressionist response, whatever the medium chosen.
2. Dance, drama and music: The poem is also rich with movement opportunities. Throughout there is the sense of flowing water which twists and turns. This should

provide a key *motif* for any work in dance. There are also the symmetrical patterns implied by the dome itself and its gardens. For characterisation in movement there are four key figures: Kubla Khan, a powerful ruler who makes the 'decree'; the 'woman wailing'; the 'demon lover' with his 'flashing eyes' and 'floating hair'; and the 'Abyssinian maid' playing her dulcimer. Any characterisations of these figures to begin with *tableaux vivants*: the child makes the living portrait of the character, perhaps in a costume, perhaps with other, invented characters. Once this is established, several more positions can be made for that character and movements from one to the other established. Using techniques developed by physical theatre, impressions of the dome, the walls and towers and other fixed objects can be made by children making group shapes with their bodies. Although there is no dialogue in the poem, speech is implied in the 'decree', the woman's 'wailing', 'ancestral voices' and the 'Abyssinian maid' who sings 'of Mount Arbora'. There is also some actual speech in the cry of 'Beware! Beware!/ His flashing eyes, his floating hair' and the following ritual chant ending in 'Paradise'. This ritual chant could be developed very effectively into a ritual song, something like a psalm. The way to do this is for the children to establish the precise rhythm of the lines by clapping and tapping, then to work out possible sounds for each beat, using the glockenspiel, xylophone, chime bars or keyboards. Another possibility for musical composition is the creation of a tone poem or film score. To do this the children should identify the key pictures or ideas in the poem, then try to make sounds that match them, using whatever instruments are available to them. For instance, 'caverns measureless to man' might involve the plucking or blowing of the lowest notes on a cello or clarinet or the slow banging of a large drum. These would obviously need to be given some simple pattern, then 'orchestrated' with *motifs* created for other key pictures. Such a tone poem could either be performed to accompany a dramatic reading of the poem or as part of a dance drama performance.

3. Performance: All of these elements together offer much for the development of a performance piece of dance, drama and music. The aim of such a piece should be to create a dance drama depicting the main elements of the poem. Involvement of this kind will clearly illuminate meanings in the poem, making the overall pursuit of literacy through poetry an exciting adventure.

A week's lessons for Year six

The Year 6 lesson notes are designed for a project which features both poetry and drama. The Shakespeare play suggested here, *The Tempest*, is one which the author has used many times before with Year 4, 5 and 6 children. As this is a major work of literature, it will be necessary at times to depart from the format followed in most of the other lesson notes. Methods of presenting the play to classes and developing work out of it will be discussed before the specific work on the 'poems' is offered.

The 'poems' chosen are two speeches and two songs as follows, and they are intended to be used by all the children, whether setted or not as the project unfolds:

'Caliban's complaint'[25] (Act 1, Scene 2)

> This island's mine, by Sycorax my mother,
> Which thou tak'st from me. When thou cam'st first,
> Thou strok'st me and made much of me, would'st give me
> Water with berries in't, and teach me how
> To name the bigger light, and how the less,
> That burn by day and night; and then I lov'd thee,
> And show'd thee all the qualities o' th' isle,
> The fresh springs, brine-pits, barren place and fertile.
> Curs'd be I that did so. All the charms
> Of Sycorax, toads, beetles, bats, light on you!
> For I am all the subjects that you have,
> Which first was mine own king; and here you sty me
> In this hard rock, whiles you keep from me
> The rest o' th' island.

'Full fathom five'[26] (Act 1, Scene 2)

> Full fathom five thy father lies;
> Of his bones are coral made;
> Those are pearls that were his eyes;
> Nothing of him that doth fade,
> But doth suffer a sea change
> Into something rich and strange.
> Sea-nymphs hourly ring his knell:
> Ding-dong,
> Hark now I hear them, ding-dong bell.

'Caliban speaks of the isle'[27] (Act 3, Scene 2)

> Be not afeard. The isle is full of noises,
> Sounds and sweet airs that give delight and hurt not.
> Sometimes a thousand twangling instruments
> Will hum about mine ears; and sometimes voices,
> That, if I then had wak'd after long sleep,
> Will make me sleep again; and then, in dreaming,
> The clouds methought would open and show riches
> Ready to drop upon me, that, when I wak'd,
> I cried to dream again.

'Where the bee sucks'[28] (Act 5, Scene 1)

> Where the bee sucks, there suck I;
> In a cowslip's bell I lie;
> There I couch when owls do cry.
> On the bat's back I do fly
> After summer merrily.
> Merrily, merrily shall I live now
> Under the blossom that hangs on the bough.

Presenting the story and text to children

Most teachers who introduce juniors to Shakespeare do so by using prose re-tellings of the story by the likes of Leon Garfield, Bernard Miles or Ian Serraillier, and this works. However, as *The Tempest* is actually a play for performance on a stage, rather than a novel for reading in the study, a more dynamic presentation of the story is better. Adventurous teachers might follow a storytelling approach with the reading of key extracts of text as they go along. Such an approach follows the structure of the work in five acts with different scenes in each act. So each scene is an episode.

To illustrate this principle let us imagine a teacher starting the project. Instead of saying "Once upon a time" or reading from Garfield, "Far, far away, upon the shore of a strange island"[29] she takes the children straight to the heart of the work by saying, "A ship is in a storm. There is 'a tempestuous noise' (from the stage directions). On board the ship there is a king and a prince, a duke and some lords, a jester, a butler, the captain and the crew. The crew can hardly control the ship. The storm is really raging and the important passengers keep getting in the way. . . . ."

The reason for this alternative approach is that it is closer to performance, closer to the nature of *The Tempest*, being delivered in the present tense. It requires, however, the teacher to prepare herself thoroughly, know each episode and to mark the key passage she wants to use. The teacher might finish the short opening scene in Act 1 by saying, "Everyone is falling in the water as the ship goes down and a wise old man called Gonzalo shouts, 'Now I would give a thousand furlongs of sea for an acre of barren ground' (Act 1, Scene 1). Yes, he would rather be anywhere on earth than here going down with the ship".

Another key to the initial success of the project will be to familiarise the children with names, relationships and status of all the main characters, and the way to do this is to make a large, clear wallchart always available and ensure that every child learns the names, how to say them and who they are, even before the first episode is told.

In the early stages of a project of this kind, the presentation will become a little discursive as the teacher asks and explains things about the story and the characters. For instance, in the second scene of Act 1, the relationship between Prospero, his brother Antonio (who stole his position) and the King of Naples, Alonso, (who helped him) will need to be carefully explained, perhaps with the use of diagrams on the board.

As the teacher gets more confident and the children more interested, the storytelling might get closer to a kind of enactment. For instance, when Prospero and his daughter Miranda go to see Caliban, the monster, the teacher might use two of the children to direct her storytelling towards the one to represent Miranda, the other Caliban. Thus the theatrical nature of the play is closer to realisation. Later still this might involve children actually learning extracts of the text to speak in reply to the teacher. Good examples of this can be found in descriptions of two projects which the author undertook in the 1980s, based on *King Lear*[30] and *Hamlet.*[31]

Encouraging initial responses

During such sessions pupils will want to make comments and should be encouraged to do so. I can remember the opening episode of my Hamlet project being concluded just before a break and none of the children wanting to go out. They had to speak, to speculate. Such enthusiasm should quickly be guided into written response. The King Lear project offers a model for this. The following simple request was made by the teacher, 'Write about a character or event or situation which stands out strongly in your mind.' The idea was that the children would not simply write the whole story back. Rather they were expected 'to focus their minds on the one moment, or short sequence of moments, like freezing a frame in a film, or like playing an action replay. A kind of meditation was induced, a reverie on the theme of the episode'.[32]

This very simple technique was applied to *The Tempest* in a subsequent project and produced the following kind of work, which was typical, whilst being individual. Here a Year 6 child writes about Caliban[33]:

> Deformed, disfigured and distorted he stands
> The son of the foul witch Sycorax
> Now commanded by Prospero and
> Miranda, his life not his own.
> He groans and cries when struck with cramp.
> And in torment stalks the land.
> The poor creature, half man, half beast
> trapped inside the body of a repulsive freak.
> His name is a whisper on mankind's lips.
> Do I dare to speak his name?
> Caliban.

Developing response to the 'poems'

Teachers will obviously need to develop a range of activities designed to develop their children's understanding of the plot or story line, the nature of the key characters and their relationships, but here I focus on activities relating to the poetry. The poetry in *The Tempest* consists mainly of the iambic pentameters spoken by noble characters. These are lines which are roughly ten syllables long and sometimes known as 'blank verse'. There are also the lyrics for songs of which 'Full fathom five' is the most well-known.

These passages should be used for literacy hour work after the teacher has told the episode in which it happens and developed initial responses to that episode. That way the children will have a context for it. As with the approaches to other poems in this chapter, the children should make a good attempt at learning the passage at home the weekend before the lessons.

'Caliban's complaint'

1. Try to memorise the speech yourself and practise speaking it as if you are Caliban, before presenting it to the children. Pin up a large poster version of the speech and

speak it to the class as dramatically as you can in role. There is a change of mood in it. Up to '. . . . . barren place and fertile' Caliban is quieter and pitiable as he recollects the relationship he had with Prospero in earlier days. Then he gets into his raging mood in which he curses Prospero. Explain this to the children, before asking them to read it, a line each, one after the other. Allow the speech to be repeated until every child has spoken a line of it. Divide the children into groups of four and repeat. Divide the class in half and repeat again. The children will thoroughly enjoy this.

2. Explain that Shakespeare has put many apostrophes in to abbreviate his words, something they will find out more about later. So 'tak'st' means 'takest' which in today's words means 'took'.

3. Maintain the groups of four for a conference. Divide the speech roughly into pairs of lines and allocate a pair to each group. Their task is to work out the meaning of their two lines. Allow only about ten minutes for this, then ask the spokesperson for each group to tell the class what the lines mean. Summarise what they say and ask them to write this in their own words.

4. Return to the vocabulary. The children should list all the words with the apostrophes in and write the modern day equivalent next to them. Ask the groups to discuss the particular use of the following words: '*by* Sycorax', '*made much* of me', '*bigger light*', '*qualities* o' th' isle', '*subjects*' and '*sty* me'. Children to list the words, their usual meanings and their rather different meanings in the speech.

5. Teach the children about the kind of poetic line used here by Shakespeare. Tell them that it is called the 'iambic pentameter' which means that it usually has ten syllables or beats. To demonstrate the rhythm, return to chanting the lines in groups with a member of each group tapping the rhythm on a tambourine or drum.

6. If this work is successful the children should examine the speech by Prospero which answers it. They will then see that Caliban has omitted to remember some important facts.

'Full fathom five'

1. Arrange the class into groups of four or so, attempting to get a good voice blend in each group, and allocate a line each with the eighth group reading from 'ding-dong' through to 'ding-dong bell'. Each group to practise the line, trying to create a soft, chantlike sound, remembering that this is Ariel singing to Ferdinand about his father's alleged death by drowning.

2. Children, individually, to write exactly what they see when they hear these lines and to make quick sketches of these pictures in their minds with a view to more developed paintings later.

3. For focused word work the children to study the following glossary: 'fathom' – unit of measurement as long as an average man's outstretched arms; 'coral' – a form of rock made by sea creatures squirting out special substances; 'sea-nymphs' – mythical creatures like fairies that live in the sea (not mermaids); 'knell' – the ringing of a bell when someone is dead; 'hark' – listen. This should clarify what they see. Ask the children in their groups to work out what these lines mean: 'Of his bones are coral

made', 'Those are pearls that were his eyes', 'Nothing of him that doth fade' and 'doth suffer a sea change'. To summarise this, ask the children what is the theme or the overall meaning of the song.

4. The children to look at the rhymes in the poem: 'lies–eyes', 'made–fade', 'change–strange' and 'knell–bell'. How are these arranged? There is a difference between the first four lines and the second. There are also differences in the way the same sounds are spelt. Children to list these facts.

5. Children to look at Shakespeare's use of alliteration: 'Full fathom five – father', 'suffer a sea change – something – strange – sea-nymphs', 'ding-dong – ding-dong'. What kind of sounds are these. Try to direct the children to see that 'f' and 's' are soft sounds which consist of releases of air but that 'd' sounds are hard. Why does Shakespeare use sounds this way?

6. An interesting lesser issue is the use of punctuation. Shakespeare makes much use of the semi-colon and comma. There are only two full stops. How does this affect the way the lines should be spoken? A semi-colon is a shorter stop than a full stop. Children to practise saying the lines with different lengths of stop as follows: comma – shortest stop; semi-colon – longer; colon – longer still; full stop – longest stop. An exciting challenge can be set to the groups to try to speak the lines showing different lengths of stop.

'Caliban speaks of the isle'

1. Use the same approach as for 'Caliban's complaint': children speaking a line each one after the other, individually then in pairs and groups. The mood and tone of 'Caliban speaks of the isle', however, is very different from that of 'Caliban's complaint'. Firstly, Caliban is trying to persuade his new 'friends' not to be afraid of the island, so the mood is quieter and gentler. However, Caliban gets carried away by his love of the island and the speech is full of ecstasy. So the voice should rise gradually away from the persuasive to the wondrous, building to a crescendo on 'I cried to dream again'. It is a remarkable speech, particularly being delivered by a character who is supposed to be base. Shakespeare puts in his mouth the language of princes and nobles – iambic pentameters.

2. Divide the class into fours and allocate two lines each for discussions. They have to try to work out exactly what their lines mean. Before they start they will need a short glossary as follows: 'afeard' – afraid; 'Be not afeard' – don't be afraid; 'airs' – tunes; 'mine' – my; 'methought' – I thought. After they have fed back to the whole class, try to establish the theme of the speech: Caliban's love of the island. Then ask the whole class what they think the 'riches' are. Ask each child to write down what Caliban would consider to be 'riches'. They must think about what they have so far seen of Caliban's nature. Ask them to write a brief summary of what the speech means.

3. For words work ask the children to look for words which are to do with the sounds of the island and to list every one as follows: 'noises', 'Sounds', 'sweet airs', 'twangling instruments', 'hum', 'voices' and 'cried'. Ask them then to divide these

into three groups: (a) nouns which are the names of sounds; (b) nouns which are the names of things that make sounds; (c) verbs. They should then add a fourth group of words which describe the effect of the sounds: 'give delight' and 'hurt not'. Ask them to say which is the only word which is harsh or discordant, trying to establish that it is Caliban's 'cried'. This points to the tragedy of Caliban, being neither truly part of the island, nor part of human society. This is a crucial fact about the play.

4. In their groups the children to look for the alliterative sounds: 'afeard – full'; 'Sounds – sweet – Sometimes – sometimes – sleep – sleep'; 'dreaming – drop – dream'. From this the children should be led to realise that the speech is soft with its 'f' and 's' sounds, that even the harder 'd' sounds are softened by being blended into 'dr' sounds. In 'Caliban's complaint' alliteration is not as prominent, but its main sound is 'b': 'berries – bigger – burn – brine-pits – barren – beetles – bats', a harder sound, which is appropriate for a harsher speech. The children should list all these alliterations.

5. The children to look at the punctuation, which is similar to that in 'Caliban's complaint'. In both speeches Caliban gets 'wound up' emotionally. This makes him speak with few major pauses for breath. Children to examine the occurrence of full stops and other punctuation marks in terms of what it shows about Caliban's emotional state. In the first speech they might notice that the passage 'When thou cam'st first' to 'barren place and fertile' is one long sentence and in the second there is a long sentence from 'Sometimes a thousand' to the end. Both passages match exactly the parts of the speeches when Caliban is more emotionally charged.

'Where the bee sucks'

1. As with 'Full fathom five' try to create groups which are like little choirs with complementary voices. 'Where the bee sucks', however, is a very different song. Whereas 'Full fathom' is sombre, this is light and merry. Remind the children that 'Full fathom' was about death by drowning whereas this is a freedom song. It is Ariel's song when he is released from his service to Prospero. In terms of sounds there is an echo running through it caused by the same rhyming sound for each of the first four lines. Each of these lines also has a sense of being divided in two as in (a) 'Where the bee sucks', (b) 'there suck I'. Ask the children, therefore, to try to speak the song with a different person's voice for each half line until they get to 'After summer' which they should speak together to the end. This will consolidate the sound pattern in their minds.

2. Ask the children to write exactly what they see, then do three or four quick sketches to capture this for later use in painting.

3. The only words that, perhaps, need a glossary are 'couch' – lie down; 'bough' – large branch of a tree. Divide the class into groups of four. This time each group should work out the meaning of the whole poem from the question 'What sort of life does Ariel think he will have after Prospero leaves?' They should be very precise in the details. Where will he go when it is dark? What will he eat? What will he do for fun? Which three places will he rest in?

4. Children in their groups to list the two sets of rhymes: 'I–lie–cry–fly' and 'now–bough'. Draw their attention to the variations of spelling of words making the same sound. Children to find other examples of these spellings and look for other spellings that make the same sounds. They should note these.
5. Children to count the syllables in each line – seven in the first five, then two tens. What effects does this have? After the children have offered ideas, establish that the last two lines summarise Ariel's new life, whereas the previous five lines give examples of it. They should also compare the punctuation with that in 'Full fathom five'. Is it similar with different kinds of stops? Repeat the exercise in which the children practise different lengths of stop when they chant the words.

Links in the arts

The arts can lead both to the understanding of meaning in a text and the expression of personal response to it. These two roles should be kept firmly in mind. Children need both. They need to comprehend the wider meanings that writers put in their texts and they need to make those meanings part of their reveries, in other words to 'see' the pictures in the texts within their own frame of reference. If the arts are to be deployed in a project of this kind, therefore, tasks need to be set which further these twin aims. The suggested tasks laid out below attempt to do this.

Art

The children will already have done sketches based on the two songs and these can provide valuable material for paintings. However, they could also be developed in different ways such as in three dimensional works, fabric-printing and painting or murals. What is to be strenuously avoided is any work which turns 'the isle' into an actual place such as designing a travel brochure or making a board-game. Such activities, which are frequent teacher responses in Shakespeare projects, go against the grain of the text. The island in *The Tempest* is an island of the pure imagination. It is not located in the Caribbean or the Mediterranean.

Suitable responses in art can also be made in response to Caliban's two speeches.

1. Ask the children to choose one of the following extracts of the text, asking them to try and 'see it', then make a quick sketch as a starting point for a more elaborate piece of work: 'When thou cam'st first' with one or more of the examples that Caliban cites; 'All charms. . . . .' with Prospero beset by one of these charms; and 'here you sty me/In this hard rock'. These will lead to more realistic, photographic kinds of work, being somewhat factual.
2. For more abstract and personal responses set the following: 'The isle is full of noises'; 'sometimes voices . . . . .'; and 'The clouds . . . . . would open and show riches'.

Dance

Confine your attention to 'Full fathom five' for work in dance, focusing on the idea of things changing into other things. This, after all, is a key theme of the whole play.

1. Start each session with warming up exercises in which the children do shape-changing exercises – from wide to narrow, tall to short, rounded to thin, alive to dead, human to rock and so on.
2. The key notion in the song is of a dead thing fading then being transformed into 'something rich and strange'. Play a movement game in which the children have to invent horrible or dull or dead things then transform them into beautiful, strange things.
3. Divide the children into groups. Provide each group with a copy of the poem and challenge them to produce a set of movements to interpret the song. This should last over a sequence of at least three lessons and should produce recognisable dances. The dances can be accompanied by recitations or singings of the song or musical pieces. (See 'Music' below.)
4. When the children have heard every episode of the play, develop the work further. Ask the groups to think of examples which show things being changed. They might, for instance, think of Ariel becoming free; Caliban getting drunk; Prospero giving up magic or Miranda falling in love. They should try to make a set of movements which show one of these changes and add it to the 'Full fathom five' dances they have made.

Drama

Unless the children are experienced at role play and working with scripts, avoid sessions in which they act out dialogue from the text itself. Instead, use drama to get deeper into the meanings of the two speeches by Caliban.

1. For warm-ups get the children making Calibans. What does he look like? How does he move? How would he speak before Prospero taught him language? Work on these three aspects of Caliban before every session.
2. Divide the children into pairs, one as Prospero and one as Caliban, taking as the theme for the exercise Caliban's recollection of what they did in the early days. Remembering that Prospero taught Caliban to speak English, the children should enact Caliban showing Prospero 'all the qualities o' th' isle' and Prospero teaching him the English words for things.
3. Focus on the idea of the 'riches' in Caliban's dream for the main part of the work. Divide the children into groups of four and ask them to make a play, using mime or speech, of Caliban's dream, which will represent the things he most wants. The children might include in it scenes when Caliban and Miranda were children, before he attacked her. They might include a scene in which he marries her. After all it is Caliban's dream!

Music

There are two kinds of musical composition that can be used, one for 'Full fathom five' and the other for 'Caliban speaks of the isle'.

1. In groups the children should be challenged to compose a tune to go with the words of 'Full fathom five'. They need to remember that the song is about death and that towards the end the sound of a death bell is heard.
2. The children should proceed as follows: (a) Speak the words out loud with expression, varying the volume and the tempo until it sounds right; (b) Tap out the rhythm made when the words are spoken this way, line by line with a beater on the table; (c) Transfer this rhythm to a glockenspiel, set of chime bars or xylophone, experimenting and discussing the tunes made and whether they are right or not; (d) Half the group speaks the words while the other half tries to fit the tune to it; (e) All the group attempts to sing the lyrics; (f) Rehearse several times then perform to others.
3. The second kind of composition is the 'tone poem' or 'film score' which is background music to highlight or illustrate something happening in the action. The children in their groups, using whatever instruments are available, should attempt a sound track for the speech. If some of them are learning to play a musical instrument, so much the better.
4. Firstly, the children need to make a sound motif to represent Caliban himself, perhaps something heavy and crude with an edge of beauty! Next they should make a sound *motif* for the island. The clue for this is in the 'twangling instruments' that 'hum'. The children will need to experiment with the production of alternative sounds for this.
5. So, the children will have two *motifs* and will need to make a pattern for them. They will need to decide which *motif* will start the composition and which will join in. Will they both continue throughout? If the children are not experienced at this sort of work, suggest that Caliban's motif opens the piece, then the island motif joins it and continues throughout while Caliban's comes in from time to time.
6. The children's tone poems should be used to accompany their plays.

Poetry-writing

The children will already be in the habit of writing poetic responses after many of the episodes the teacher tells to them. Poetry-writing in addition to this should offer them the opportunity to speculate beyond the text towards its implications. The following offers a range of possibilities for this:

1. Imagine the time when Caliban first saw Prospero, before they actually met. Perhaps he sees Prospero and his daughter coming ashore from their little boat. Write some lines, if possible with ten syllables in each one, which describe what he saw and how he felt, that will fit into the speech.
2. Imagine King Alonso drowning and 'suffer(ing) a sea-change'. Think of different parts of him. What do they change into? Use Shakespeare's way of writing the song and add eight lines to it about Alonso changing.

3. Write a poem about Caliban's dream and its riches.

4. Imagine other things that Ariel might do now he is free. In the song there are only a small number of examples. Add another four lines with seven syllables in each and, if possible, with rhymes at the end of each line.

Finally, provide plenty of opportunity for children to share their work in performances and exhibitions.

References

1. Stannard, J. (1998ii) *The National Literacy Strategy, Framework for Teaching*, The National Literacy Project, Reading.

2. Carter, D. (1998) 'Storm' in *Sleeplessness Jungle*, CPP, Mold.

3. Carter, D. (1998) 'It was Cat' in *Sleeplessness Jungle*, CPP, Mold.

4. Anonymous, 'Key to the Kingdom' in Opie, I. and Opie, P. (Eds) *The Oxford Nursery Rhyme Book*, OUP, Oxford.

5. Carter, D. (1998) 'Blessings' in *Sleeplessness Jungle*, CPP, Mold.

6. Carter, D. (1998) 'Up here' in *Sleeplessness Jungle*, CPP, Mold.

7. Anonymous, 'I saw a peacock' in Opie, I. and Opie, P. (Eds) *The Oxford Nursery Rhyme Book*, OUP, Oxford.

8. Anonymous, 'What's in there?' in Opie, I. and Opie, P. (Eds) *The Oxford Nursery Rhyme Book*, OUP, Oxford.

9. Anonymous, 'There I saw' in Opie, I. and Opie, P. (Eds) *The Oxford Nursery Rhyme Book*, OUP, Oxford.

10. Carter, D. (1998) 'Ed's Head' in *Sleeplessness Jungle*, CPP, Mold.

11. Reeves, J. 'The Sea' (1950) in *The Wandering Moon*, Heinemann, London.

12. Longfellow, H.W. 'The tide rises, the tide falls' in Walters, F. (Ed) (1985) *Golden Apples*, Macmillan, London.

13. Curnow, A. 'Wild Iron' in Heaney, S. and Hughes, T. (Eds) (1984) *The Rattle Bag*, Faber, London.

14. Moore, L. 'Until I saw the sea' in Walters, F. (Ed.) (1985) *Golden Apples*, Macmillan, London.

15. Clare, J. 'Little Trotty Wagtail' in Tibble, J.W. and Tibble, A. (Eds) (1976) *Selected Poems*, Dent, London.

16. Lear, E. 'The Pelican Chorus' in Grigson, G. (Ed.) (1979) *The Faber Book of Nonsense Verse*, Faber, London.

17. Tennyson, Lord 'The Owl' in (1953) *The Faber Book of Children's Verse*, Faber, London.

18. Grahame, K. 'Ducks' Ditty' in Philip, N. (Ed.) (1996) *The New Oxford Book of Children's Verse*, OUP, Oxford.

19. cummings, e.e. 'in Just-' (1953) in *Tulips and Chimneys*, Liveright, New York.

20. Keats, J. 'Meg Merrilies' (1955) in *The Poems of John Keats*, Collins, London.

21. Carter, D. (1998) 'Old Man' in *Sleeplessness Jungle*, CPP, Mold.

22. Jennings, E. (1966) 'The Ugly Child', in *The Secret Brother*, Macmillan, London.

23. Carter, D. (1994) *Imagined Worlds Project Report*, CPP, Mold.

24. Coleridge, S.T. 'Kubla Khan', in Beer, J.B. (Ed.) (1963) *Selected Poems*, Dent, London.

25. Shakespeare, W. 'This island's mine . . . . .', *The Tempest*, in *The Complete Works of William Shakespeare*, Collins, London.

26. Ibid, 'Be not afeard . . . . .'

27. Ibid. 'Full fathom five . . . . .'

28. Ibid. 'Where the bee sucks . . . . .'
29. Garfield, L. (1985) *Shakespeare Stories*, Gollancz, London.
30. Carter, D. (Spring 1986) 'King Lear in the Junior Classroom', *English in Education*, Vol. 20, No. 1, NATE, Sheffield.
31. Carter, D. (Summer 1989) 'A Country Discovered', *Cambridge Journal of Education*, Vol. 19, No. 3, Cambridge Institute of Education, Cambridge.
32. Carter, D. (1991) *The isle is full of noises*, Clwyd County Council, Mold.
33. Ibid.

Chapter Five:

Dreams and the Imagination

Children's thinking

It is the discovery of coherent speech that first makes it possible for children to let us know what they are thinking. Even then we only have occasional glimpses of that stream of conscious and unconscious thought and perception which is part of everybody's being. Children are more likely to use speech in various social interactions than to communicate thoughts which have no motives in physical need. Most children will quite spontaneously give us access to their speculations, but they are less likely to do this in a context of question–answer with an adult. It is as the French poet, Rene Char, once wrote: 'No bird can sing in a thicket of questions'.[1]

The wise adult will, therefore, allow young children control over the agenda of their conversation and respond in ways which praise and validate the child's communication of thought. Thus the grandfather shows delight when his three-year-old grand-daughter looks into his face, particularly at his spectacles, and says, "If you didn't have ears, you wouldn't be able to wear those glasses, would you?" Had that grandfather asked "What are ears for?" it is unlikely that such a perception would have emerged, unless the child had thought of it before, for such an observation is the outward sign of that child's being in a state of reverie.

In his book *The Poetics of Reverie*, Gaston Bachelard observes: 'The subconscious is ceaselessly murmuring and it is by listening to these murmurs that one hears the truth'. Reverie, usually referred to by the rather disparaging term 'day-dreaming', is the state of being 'lost in thought' and is generally looked down upon. It is seen as being something that people who are 'out of touch with reality' engage in. Yet it is unlikely that any of the great buildings, inventions, social arrangements and systems would have been made without it. Bachelard goes on to claim that the reading and writing of literature *require* the individual to enter a state of reverie. He writes: 'Poetic images stimulate our reverie; they melt into our reverie because the power of assimilation is so great. We were reading and now we are dreaming.'[2]

Now this is a far cry from regarding literature as a purely 'logical' transaction. If Bachelard is right, the activity of reading in school should be seen in a new light. It also makes the writing of poetry a very different activity from that proposed in the many how-to-do-it books which have emerged over the last fifteen or so years. For instance, here are Pie Corbett and Brian Moses on how to teach children to write poems:

> What we have to do is to train our children to become word-searchers, to actually show them how we filter words through our minds and select the most suitable one. So, we begin by prompting the children to offer us words to describe an experience and we collect these words on the blackboard.[3]

The activity suggested here is similar to that of the crossword puzzle or word-search and is symptomatic of an attitude towards poetry in education in which technique is over-emphasised. It gives words themselves pre-eminence as if they will lead us willy-nilly to objects known as poems. Anyone engaged as a teacher-trainer or adviser for English will have seen such lessons, which place the emphasis too heavily upon the playing of word-games rather than the creation of the new worlds which are poems. As a main approach to teaching poetry-writing it is likely to lead to a transitory notion of what poetry is and emphasise a use of language estranged from feeling. It may lead to poetry being seen by children as merely a more entertaining kind of language-function and force songs from birds who do not know what their song is.

Reverie and imagination

In a way such approaches to the teaching of poetry-writing reflect a lack of trust in the perceptual worlds of children. The centre of interest is the teacher's or poet's rather than the child's notion of what a poem is. Such practise certainly doesn't see childhood for what it is, a time in our lives when our perceptions are particularly clear and full of wonder. Even in this somewhat tarnished age Bachelard's elevated view of childhood holds good: 'There are moments in childhood when every child is the astonishing being, the being who realises the astonishment of being.'[4]

It is as if we have lost faith in our children to rediscover and renew the world. It is also as if their relationship with the world is not as important as their development of skills. We don't appear to desire to teach our children actually to love the world. In this we are in danger of harming our children's futures. As Bachelard writes: 'By certain of its traits, childhood lasts all through life. It returns to animate broad sections of adult life'.[5]

If, in our teaching, even of something as important as poetry, we reduce this facility for wonder, we are in danger of adversely affecting whole lives. Bachelard sees a central role for poetry in the development of a wholesome, loving relationship with the world. He calls it 'a synthesising force for human existence' and sees its great archetypes or themes as 'reserves of enthusiasm, which help us believe in the world, love the world, create the world'.[6]

So, the making of poetry is a far more important act than merely playing games with words, even though such activities should be part of every child's education. We should, therefore, aim not so much to teach children how to write poetry as validate for them the reveries they already have or can have. We validate through response and through praise. Of praise Bachelard writes: 'When the forces of matter must be awakened, praise is sovereign. Let us remember that praise has a magical action'.[7]

We need to let children know not only that we are interested in what they are thinking and dreaming but that we also admire their thoughts and their dreams. When we are able to do this, huge forces are certainly released in most children. This is where the current interest in 'pupils' self-esteem' should have its main focus. Consider, for instance, the sense of self-esteem present in the following poem written by a Year 6 child, Paul Jackson, for his teacher, with whom he had shared many poems over two years. In it the child celebrates poetry itself:

Poems
A new world is being created
in your mind.
A dream that cannot be broken
by man or beast.
Your eyes search the object for ideas.
They write in your mind the poem.
Later the mind turns out
a masterpiece of words.

This poem's self-assurance was brought about by being written out of the child's need to make a statement to his teacher and was the result of no lesson, but was presented to the teacher on the day the child was leaving the primary school. It also rightly places the dream or concept first and the language which eventually embodies it second. The 'new world' forms before it has expression. It is a 'dream that cannot be broken' before moving into words.

Children, of course, will engage in acts of reverie without needing help from their teachers. Indeed, entering a state of reverie is a unilateral act in the classroom, although children are seldom aware that they are doing it. When detected by authority it is usually treated as subversive. They are more likely to be reprimanded than praised for 'day-dreaming'. I am reminded of one child, Tony, aged ten and new to the school, who would spend long periods simply gazing into space. He quickly acquired a reputation as a lazy, gormless sort of boy. Yet here is the outcome of one of his musings by the local river:

The river
runs away smoothly,
hides by bends,
never stops to nap,
carrying grass
also reflections
combed by rock.

Here, in seven taut little lines, we glimpse the witty, delicate mind of a child whose reveries were misunderstood. Fortunately, his teacher was able to mobilise this natural tendency to muse and he went on to write many poems, and grew in confidence as someone empowered.

Developing imagination in the classroom

Few teachers would seriously contemplate day-dreaming as a valid curricular strategy. Many, however, facilitate this power in their daily work in class without, perhaps, recognising this confidence-building, self-assuring aspect of it. Those teachers who habitually engage their pupils' imaginations strongly are almost certain to be cultivating reverie positively. The child absorbed fully in drawing or dancing, making music or in role, writing a story or a poem is drawing on a state of reverie, particularly if something new is being made.

When children make poetry in the primary school the evidence of reverie will often lie in a particular way of seeing, which can be called visionary or playful. It is frequently revealed in a line or two rather than in a whole piece. For instance, in this piece about the month of June a Year 6 child, Nigel, writes:

> The hawthorn whispers to his tall
> friend the sycamore, "Whisha. Whisha. Whisha."

and I would claim this as a product of a reverie in which trees are conscious. On the other hand, when the same child in the same piece writes:

> The white blossom hanging on the branches
> like snow.

I think it is fair to say that he has left the state of reverie and is, as it were, going through the motions of writing a poem. In this second quotation he is trying to describe a part of the tree by using a simple and, in fact, well-worn simile. In the first, on the other hand, he has had some kind of vision or the sighting of a more imaginary relationship.

In this next poem a Year 5 child, Helen, is contemplating a piece of dead ivy wood, which has been taken off an oak tree. It is dusty and riddled with worm-holes. The child makes no overt attempt to describe the wood, but enters immediately into this reverie:

> An old crooked man, dragging his feet
> as he walks through the wet lanes.
> He goes to his dusty old home
> and climbs up his dirty staircase.
> He goes to sleep with a crumpled sheet
> on him like contours off a map.

In presenting her 'day-dream' about the ivy wood the child does describe it. She follows all of its main movements and shapes but in an ingenious narrative. In so doing, she goes well beyond the appearance of the piece of wood and into sympathy – sympathy for the wood *as* the imaginary old man. Surely, she is doing exactly what Bachelard means when he writes: 'We cannot love water, fire, the tree without putting a love into them, a friendship which goes back to our childhood.'[8] We are in the end brought out of the reverie with the strangely fitting and final simile of 'contours off a map', which somehow restores the sense of an inanimate object.

Such writing cannot be 'prescribed', and adopting reverie as a deliberate teaching strategy is fraught with difficulties, particularly with older children. Most of them expect their school writing tasks to be logical, transactional and goal-orientated, even their poetry-writing tasks. So, there are no easy recipes for teachers, but there are rich rewards for them in attempting to cultivate reverie as a positive stimulus to children's writing.

A good teacher will no doubt adopt attitudes towards her pupils and develop routines which encourage their reveries and the development of their imaginations. However, there is also a need for more precise strategies to achieve simple objectives in such developments. To serve this need Clwyd Poetry Project has devised a series of 'exercises' or 'improvisations'. These are partly adaptations of old approaches and partly newly invented ones. They are all developments of the crucial first learning objective listed in Chapter Three, '1. To use imagination actively in a range of situations'.

These exercises are intended to be used regularly, almost every day, and children are expected to write intensively for no more than five minutes at a time. Children who have trouble with their writing should use the teacher or a helper to scribe for them. Each exercise is presented using the words the teacher is intended to say to the children.

Exercise 1: Recall or create dreams. Close eyes. Think of nothing if you can. Imagine you are asleep at night. You are dreaming, a long dream. I wonder what is in your dream. Where are you? What do you see? Start dreaming. Really dream or remember a dream you have had. Start writing your dream.

Exercise 2: Recall memories. Close eyes. Think back as far as you can. Right back to when you were small. Think back to your earliest memory. Write what you remember – not as a story – just the key things. Write a verse or line for each thing in that memory.
OR Think of something, anything long ago. Something about you. Something you heard or felt. Try now to see it, to make a picture of it in your mind. Try to see the picture very clearly just as if it is a picture on the wall or TV. When the picture is crystal clear inside your mind, write it as a sort of poem. In other words, put that picture outside of your mind as a poem.

Exercise 3: Listen to recorded sounds/music. Close eyes and listen to this music. Imagine you are somewhere. Listen again. What do you see? Write it as a few lines of a poem. What is happening? Write that, too, but not like a story. Write it as another few lines of your poem. Listen once again, to more of it this time. Keep writing your poem.
OR When you hear this music, pretend you are in some strange place. What do you see, hear, touch? Write what is there and what happens, but not as a story. Write it as lines in a poem.

Exercise 4: Present fairy tale or mythical images or ideas. Close eyes. Make your mind go blank. I am going to say *three words*, which I want you to imagine vividly. Imagine those three things. Write what you imagine, not as a story but as a poem.

a) Fairy tale options: king – forest – magic bird; lost – goblin – cottage; stepmother – night – water; lord – mountains – gold.

b) Mythical options: god – quest – magic ring; hero – tasks – monster; wounded – messenger – elixir.

c) Legendary options: cobbler – fairy – dawn; stream – broken crock – spirit; cockerel – pearl – traveller.

OR I will give you the name of a character out of a fairy tale (myth or legend) and I want you to imagine it and describe it in a poem.

a) Fairy characters: troll, goblin, dwarf, elf, nixie, pixie, kobold, banshee, sylph, sprite, undine.

b) Mythical characters: God, hero, mortal, monster.

c) Legend characters: underdog, trickster, Roarer, Brawler, changeling.

Exercise 5: Present evocative lines from poems. Close eyes. Make your mind go blank. I am going to speak some lines, which I want you to imagine vividly. Really try to see what the lines suggest. Add a new line of your own. When you have added one new line, write as many more as you can.
Some options:

a) 'The sedge has wither'd from the lake'[9]

b) 'When through forgotten woods dark winter breathes'[10]

c) 'in the forests of the night'[11]

d) 'Over the evening forest
   the bronze moon climbs to its place'[12]

e) '. . . . . driving veils
   of squall moved down like night on land and sea'[13]

f) 'It was getting dark in a gaping landscape'[14]

g) 'The house
   Rang like some fine green goblet'[15]

Exercise 6: Tell or read fairy tale, myth or legend. Close eyes. Make your mind go blank. Hansel and Gretel are in the woods as it goes dark. They have been abandoned by their father. Their stepmother wanted them killed. Imagine the woods just as day is turning into night – dusk – what can you see? What can you hear, feel? What are they like? Write what you can see, vividly and in short, descriptive phrases rather than like a story.

Exercise 7: Show an evocative painting or drawing. Look at this picture and pretend you can walk into it just if it has magic frame, or as if it has powers like the wardrobe in *The Lion, the Witch and the Wardrobe*. Walk in slowly and don't let yourself be seen. Write your first impression as a poem not as a story. Go in further into the middle part. What do you feel? Write it. What do you hear? Write that. What do you see? What is it like? Describe it. Go into the background. Write another impression. (This will vary greatly according to the picture.)

Exercise 8: Present archetypal images in simple, evocative language. Close eyes. Make your mind go blank. I am going to say something which I want you to imagine. I want you to try to actually see it . . . . . (see below) Now that you have seen it I want you to try to write it – not in single words nor as if you are writing a story but in single, vivid lines, one after the other.
a) How the universe was made (the world, plants, animals, people . . . . .).
b) How the world was saved from destruction (the country, the town, village, human race . . . . .).
c) How he/she was born again (born not from a woman).
d) How the great city was begun.
e) Argument (fight, battle) between father and son (mother-daughter, father-daughter, mother-son).
f) Being unable to move when you badly need to (becalmed).
g) A night journey.
h) The cavern in the high mountain.
i) Sparkling fountain.
j) Heaven and Hell (or Underworld).
k) Moon-goddess; earth-goddess; sun-god.
l) God; Saviour; ruler; all-seeing eye.

Using poets' work

In Chapter Four of this book, 'Literacy Hour Lessons', the agenda for the children's actions is set by the texts of the various poets. So Year 5 children, for instance, operate within a world created by Coleridge, the strange world of 'Kubla Khan'. This agenda is also set to a great extent by the literacy objectives identified in the follow-up activities. In that particular example – 'Kubla Khan' – the world is so conceptually and linguistically rich that its value for Year 5 children reaches beyond those literacy objectives. What the children will follow here is Coleridge's poetic reverie. They will follow a certain track, as they will in all of the poems that they encounter this way. These tracks, in Bachelard's words, are the tracks 'an expanding consciousness follows' and it is the potential of poetry for 'expanding' our 'consciousness' which is its first value for us. It should also be the main reason for developing literacy skills in the first place.[16]

The implication of Bachelard's notion of 'expanding consciousness' is that *all* thinking and feeling abilities might expand, including the facility with which the child draws from his subconscious through acts of reverie. If this is the case, then the kinds of activity described in Chapter Four will have a lasting effect on the quality of the consciousnesses of most children participating in them. Much depends on the quality of the poems themselves, which in turn depends upon the integrity of the reverie which the poet engages in.

A fundamental aspect of the expansion of children's consciousness through poetry will be in their own writing. Essentially, the activities promoted in Chapter Four are mainly acts of reading, including the writing down of words and sounds in word books. Only when children make art in some form will they step outside of the reading role and become makers in their own right. By becoming makers of poetry within the reveries of poets children will expand their powers as writers. The biographies of most great poets are proof of this. At the age of twelve Alexander Pope was already playing with the hexameters of Homer, an activity which led to the development of his own rhyming couplets used to devastating effect in such satires as 'The Rape of the Lock'.[17] Coleridge was so steeped from early childhood in his reading of the great masters of the past that his everyday thoughts were almost poems, and we have already seen Keats' debt to Spenser and Heaney's to Hopkins in Chapter Two of the book.

In our own century two great poets stand out in this respect, T. S. Eliot and Ezra Pound. So enormous was the sheer quantity and range of their readings that they were able to use the forms and nuances from them to make their own 'signatures' through them. Eliot's 'The Waste Land' is obvious and spectacular evidence of this, but so are Pound's translations. His translations of Anglo-Saxon, Chinese, Provençal and early Italian poems are creative acts rather than the mere conversion of foreign texts into English. In his introduction to Pound's *Selected Poems* T. S. Eliot puts it this way:

> In each of the elements or strands there is something of Pound and something of some other, not further analysable; the strands go to make the rope, but the rope is not yet complete. And good translation like this is not merely translation, for the translator is giving the original through himself, and finding himself through the original[18].

In translating old poems Pound created new ones.

This is an interesting phenomenon in its own right but my use of it here is intended as further justification for an approach to developing children as writers of poetry, which some might reject. It is the idea of the translator adding strands of himself to the works of others through the act of translating which interests me here. Although strictly-speaking children will not be engaged in any kind of formal act of translation, when they write within, say, the context of 'Kubla Khan', there is a sense in which they tease out strands of Coleridge and add strands of themselves to make something new. Here is an example of this from ten-year-old Michael, who had worked on the poem in dance prior to writing. In it the child imagines the 'Abyssinian maid':

> She sits in a chair of rich furs,
> playing at her dulcimer.
> A dreamer. A black mermaid.
> The sea bows to her.
> The ship drifts into the cave.
> Sea rages.
> Her ship floats into the giant iceberg.
> She changes her tune.
> No life, just subtle notes.
> A raylight shows through.
> It smells beautiful.
> It is too much for words.

In this poem the child has engaged in a reverie first brought to him by Coleridge via a sensitive, imaginative teacher. The reverie is his own, as is his expression of it. In this sense it is separate from Coleridge's work. In this sense, too, the child has complete ownership of it. His engagement with Coleridge's reverie has enabled him to have one of his own and thus expand his consciousness.

What I am recommending in this book is that teachers deliberately attempt to develop their children's dreaming potential and their skills in expressing what they experience in their reveries. I am claiming that, by so doing, they will enable the children to use their imaginations easily and facilitate reading, writing and the expansion of the consciousness. I am suggesting that teachers may go some way to achieving this by regularly using the eight kinds of exercise described above and by engaging them productively in the reveries of the poets who have gone before. In the next two sections I attempt to outline lesson patterns in which whole poems or extracts of poems are used for these purposes.

Projects for Key Stage 1

It is not the intention in this part of the book to create more poetry literacy hour lessons with shared text, word and sentence work, group work and plenary sessions. This has been done in Chapter Four. Rather it is the intention to indicate routes or tracks which teachers and students might follow using poetry to achieve the kinds of aims discussed immediately above. For each key stage there are three projects: two for developing writing and one for developing response across the arts.

Project 1: 'The Door'

Introduction

Many older poetry lovers will perhaps remember in the sixties coming across a series of books which changed their perceptions about the possibilities of poetry. This set of books was published by Penguin and called 'Penguin Modern European Poets'. I can remember being feverish with excitement in the S.P.C.K. Bookshop in Chester picking up volumes by Popa, Enzensburger, Herbert, Apollinaire, Prevert and, best of all, Miroslav Holub from Czechoslovakia in February 1969!

Holub's poem 'The Door' has since become very popular for use with children of all ages in schools and quite rightly. Its appeal is instant and this is because, like those exercises under 'Exercise 8' above, it has archetypal significance for all people, in all times, in all places. It powerfully evokes the idea of opening an unknown door which can lead to anything. All people have night dreams in which they have to open a door along a corridor with many choices of door. Holub's poem has significance for this.

Purpose: To develop poetry-writing
Length of time: A week

Focus: 'The Door'[19]

> Go and open the door.
> Maybe outside there's
> a tree, or a wood,
> a garden,
> or a magic city.
>
> Go and open the door.
> Maybe a dog's rummaging.
> Maybe you'll see a face,
> or an eye,
> or the picture
> of a picture.
>
> Go and open the door.
> If there's a fog
> it will clear.
>
> Go and open the door.
> Even if there's only
> the darkness ticking,
> even if there's only
> the hollow wind,
> even if
> nothing
> is there,
> go and open the door.
>
> At least
> there'll be
> a draught.

Preparation

1. Pin a large poster version of the poem on the classroom wall and have smaller copies available for the children.
2. Practise reading the poem out loud, trying to develop a quiet, clear and mysterious recitation of it.

Stage One

1. Read the poem out loud to the children. Allow them to think for a moment before saying anything. Then ask the children to close their eyes and try to see the door and what might be through it while you read the poem to them again.
2. Say to them, "I wonder what is behind the door. Close your eyes again. What do *you* see through *your* door?"
3. If the children are not confident writers they should say what they see to a scribe. Otherwise they should write down what they see very briefly at this stage.

4. They might give answers like these, which are from one group of children: 'A little house in a garden', 'A city that is made of gold', and 'An owl sitting in a tree'. Lines such as these should be written in books as possible titles for poems.

5. Ask the children to read the poem out loud, each one reading a single line even if it consists of one word only. Do this several times so that they have the opportunity of speaking a number of different lines.

6. Ask the children to close their eyes again and try to see something else through their door. Repeat this several times, recording what they see each time.

Stage Two

1. If the children are very young or ones who cannot write, make a class poem, using each child's best line. This might imitate Holub's structure as in Rebecca's:

> Go and open the door.
> Maybe outside there's
> a little house in a garden,
> a city that is made of gold
> or an owl sitting in a tree.

2. Alternatively, you might compile the poem as if it is an answer to the mystery of what is behind the door, like this:

> Outside the door there's
> a little house in a garden,
> a city that is made of gold
> and an owl sitting in a tree.

3. You might decide to do several compilations and talk to the children about all the different ways that ideas and pictures can be made in a poem. Make these into posters and pin them alongside the Holub original. Read them to the children.

4. Ask the children to close their eyes and think about the best thing they saw behind the door. Say to them, "I want you to pretend that you are opening that door and going into that favourite place of yours. When you are in there look around. What do you see? What do you hear?"

5. The children then either write about what is on the other side of the door or tell a scribe. Keep urging the children to go further into their favourite place behind the door, describing all the things they see there. The aim should be to build considerable pieces of writing.

6. If the children are confident writers they should move more quickly from Stage One to the writing of their own poems. They will not need to be involved in whole class poems.

7. The children's poems might be word-processed onto a disk and made into a book with a copy printed out for each child. This will then enable them to have access to one another's work. Alternatively, they might copy them out in their best handwriting and put them into a class book, which becomes part of the general collection of books.

Project 2: Day, night and dreams

Purpose: To develop poetry-writing
Length of time: Three weeks

Week One Focus: 'Hide and Seek'[20]

> Hide and seek, says the Wind,
> In the shade of the woods;
> Hide and seek, says the Moon,
> To the hazel buds;
> Hide and seek, says the Cloud,
> Star on to star;
> Hide and seek, says the Wave
> At the harbour bar;
> Hide and seek, say I,
> To myself, and step
> out of the dream of Wake
> Into the dream of sleep.

Movement work

1. Warming up: When they have found their own spaces ask the children to make open and closed shapes and large and small shapes. Then ask them to make open and closed movements and large and small movements.
2. Hide and Seek:
   - Develop shapes and movements work to explore the themes of 'Hide and Seek': wind-shape; moon-shape; cloud-shape; wave-shape; wind-movement; moon-movement; cloud-movement; wave-movement.
   - Ask the children to say the words 'hide and seek' as the wind, moon, cloud, and wave would say them. Ask half of the class to make the shapes and movements of woods, buds, stars and the sea while the others speak the words 'hide and seek' to each of these things in turn.
3. Calming down: Say to the children "Be yourself asleep after all these dreams, tucked up safely in bed. Then I am waking you up. When I wake you, go and quietly get changed."

Choral speaking, conversing and group composition

1. Pin up a poster version of de la Mare's 'Hide and Seek' and read it to the children while they follow.
2. Divide the class into three groups, dividing each verse into three parts: one group says 'Hide and seek' each time; another says, 'says the Wind/Cloud/Wave/I'; and the third group says the line about who the 'hide and seek' is said to. Repeat this twice, with the groups changing parts both times.
3. Divide each of the three groups into two sub-groups and ask the sub-groups briefly

to decide what else might say 'hide and seek', while the other sub-group listens. When the decision is made the second sub-group should decide who the 'hide and seek' might be said to.

4. If this works properly there should be three new verses for the poem to be added to the poster, as in the following examples:

> Hide and seek says the Sun
> to the warm silver sand.
>
> Hide and seek says the Tree
> in the hot summer land.
>
> Hide and seek says the Rain
> to the owl's flapping wing.

Individual composition

1. Ask the children what they think is the difference between a 'dream of sleep' and a 'dream of wake'. Invite examples, attempting to involve as many children as possible.
2. Finish the week's work by getting the class meditating on the two kinds of dreams. Say, "I want you to close your eyes and think of a dream you had when asleep in bed. What do you remember? What do you see, hear, feel, smell and touch? Write that. Keep writing that as much as you can."
3. Do the same for a dream of day. Say to the class, "Close your eyes and let your mind wander anywhere it wants to. I wonder where your mind has wandered to. Wherever it has gone, write about that. Keep writing about that as much as you can."

Week Two Focus: 'Windy Nights'[21]

> Whenever the moon and stars are set,
> Whenever the wind is high,
> All night long in the dark and wet,
> A man goes riding by.
> Late in the night when the fires are out,
> Why does he gallop and gallop about?
>
> Whenever the trees are crying aloud
> And ships are tossed at sea,
> By, on the highways, low and loud,
> By at the gallop goes he.
> By at the gallop he goes, and then
> By he comes back at the gallop again.

Movement

1. Warming up: Children recollect their shapes and movements of the previous week: wind-shape; moon-shape; cloud-shape; wave-shape; wind-movement; moon-movement; cloud-movement; wave-movement.
2. Windy Nights:
   - Children to make their wind-shapes again then to change them so that they are those of strong winds. Try to get the children to produce a range of shapes for different strengths of wind.
   - Ask them next to make their wind-movements again and change them so that they are strong winds. Get the children to produce a range of different strengths of wind from breeze to gale.
   - Children to make the shape of a man galloping on a horse, then to gallop fast around the hall, avoiding bumping into one another. Repeat this, using a group of about five children to make galloping sounds using drums, tom-toms, coconut shells and tambourines. Allow different groups to play the instruments.
   - Children to make the shapes of different kinds of trees in the wind and to move like them. Try to get a good variety of shapes and movements. Ask them to make the sound that trees make in the wind as they make their movements, quietly at first but getting louder.
   - Children in groups of three or four to make the shape of a boat, then to make the boat move on the sea. Ask them to make the shape of a boat in a storm, then to make it move like a boat in the sea in a storm.
   - Put all these shapes and movements together into a performance as follows: a) a group of gallopers; b) a group of instrumentalists; c) a group of trees in the wind, who also make the sounds; d) a group of tossing boats in a storm at sea. Arrange the groups so that the gallopers can go 'by at the gallop' then 'back at the gallop again.'
3. Calming down: Ask the children to lie down as if they are the children listening to all this from their bedroom window. They should imagine that the wind has died down. Ask them to dream about a stormy night they can remember. Allow sufficient time for this, then let them go to get changed in twos and threes.

Speaking and conversation

1. Read out the new version of 'Hide and Seek' to the children telling them how well they made new lines for the poem the previous week. Briefly talk to them about their individual poems, too.
2. Pin up the poster version of Stevenson's 'Windy Nights'. Read it to them and get them to join in on every line in which the word 'gallop' appears.
3. Divide the children into groups of three or four and ask them to discuss who or what they think is the galloping man. Ask them also to find clues which tell them that it happens at night.

Individual writing

1. As soon as the children return to the class ask them to remember what they saw in their stormy night dream then to write it.
2. Ask the children what the wind did in their dream and write a few lines about it. Then repeat by asking what the trees did and what the boats did. Ask them to describe vividly what they did and add them to the stormy night dream poem.
3. The children should now read their work. Can they make it better? How? Children to improve their work as far as they can.

Week Three Focus: 'Dream Poem'[22]

> I have not seen this house before.
> Yet room for room I know it well:
> A thudding clock upon the stair,
> A mirror slanted on the wall.
>
> A round-pane giving on the park.
> Above the hearth a painted scene
> Of winter huntsmen and the pack.
> A table set with fruit and wine.
>
> Here is a childhood book, long lost.
> I turn its wasted pages through:
> Every word I read shut fast
> In a far tongue I do not know.
>
> Out of a thinness in the air
> I hear the turning of a key
> And once again I turn to see
> The one who will be standing there.

Movement

1. Warming up: Repeat movements from previous week: the wind movements, the tree movements, the galloping movements and the boat movements. Try to repeat the whole class performance which finished last week's lesson.
2. Dreaming:
   - Allow sufficient time for the children to do this. They should then lie down and imagine they are in their beds back at home. They wake up in the middle of the night. It is very dark.
   - Ask them to get up and look in the nearest mirror. What do they see? Ask them to look through their bedroom window. What do they see? Ask them to remember what they saw for later.
   - Ask them to pretend they can hear sounds downstairs. What do they hear? Then they walk slowly downstairs without putting on the light. They go into the main

room downstairs. What is hanging on the wall? What do they see on a cupboard, shelf or table?

- The children in their night walking find something on the floor from long, long ago when they were very young. What is it? They hear a door opening. Who or what comes in?

3. Calming down: The children then pretend to return to bed and go back to sleep. Tell them you will wake them up for school and do so by touching them. They then go and get changed.

Speaking and conversation

1. Pin up the poster version of Causley's 'Dream Poem'. Read it to the children, then divide them into four speaking groups and allocate one verse to each.
2. Ask the children to practise reading out their verse in the best possible way and to work out what it means. Allow the use of dictionaries and make sure you are available to join in the discussions. It would be advantageous also to have some helpers in this classroom session.
3. The children to recite their verses one after the other to make a whole poem recitation, then a member of each group to tell the class what they think their verse means.

Individual writing.

1. Having explored their houses in that night walking sequence in movement, the children should now be asked to repeat the exercise in their imaginations and write it.
2. Take them once again through the rooms sequence to see if 'room for room' they know their houses well. Put great stress on what they see in their mirrors and through their windows. This might prove to be useful as in these examples: 'I went to the window – the garden came alive'; 'A bat was flying in the air. It looked wise'; 'Through the window a pony crossing the rainbow'.
3. The children's whole poems might look something like this by Adam:

> A glass smashed onto a box,
> a rusty swing with weary
> string on. A reflection of me.
> A picture of King James the First
> we got at a jumble sale.
> A glass of water in the centre
> of the table. Holey pyjamas
> left from years ago. A door
> suddenly starts to creak open.
> Silently and out of the door
> came a black cat.

Project 3: 'Overheard on a Saltmarsh'

Purpose: To develop response to poetry across the arts
Length of project: Six weeks or half a term

Focus: 'Overheard on a Saltmarsh'[23]

> Nymph, nymph, what are your beads?
> *Green glass, goblin. Why do you stare at them?*
> Give them me.
> *No.*
> Give them me. Give them me.
> *No.*
>
> Then I will howl all night in the reeds,
> Lie in the mud and howl for them.
> *Goblin, why do you love them so?*
>
> They are better than stars or water,
> Better than voices of winds that sing,
> Better than any man's fair daughter,
> Your green glass beads on a silver ring.
> *Hush, I stole them out of the moon.*
>
> Give me your beads, I desire them.
> *No.*
> I will howl in a deep lagoon
> For your green glass beads, I love them so.
> Give them me. Give them me.
> *No.*

Preparation

1. Make a large poster and smaller copies of Monro's poem.
2. Practise reading the poem so that you develop your best possible performance for the children. Pay particular attention to where you place the emphasis of your voice, how you can vary the volume and how you make the sounds of two voices.

Stage One: Drama and movement

1. Warm the children up by asking them to make small and large shapes, thin and plump shapes, light and heavy shapes and to move slowly then quickly from one to the other. Try to get the children to transform from one to the other in an unbroken sequence of movement.
2. Pair them and ask them to imagine that one of them has something wonderful which the other one wants. Without using words and without touching, one makes asking gestures and the other makes refusing gestures. Challenge the children to produce,

say, three different asking gestures and three complementary refusing gestures. The movements must look like they go together as ask/refuse. Build up the urgency of this by saying that the askers become demanders and the refusers become defenders. Let the children swap roles several times.

3. Make a circle and ask the pupils to sit. Ask them to talk about what things were so wonderful and how it felt to want and how it felt to refuse. Ask them also what words might they have used, if allowed, in this game. After they have exhausted the possibilities, pair them again. This time ask them to keep their gestures and add words, words of asking and words of refusing. Challenge them to try and speak their groups of words with beats or rhythms in their voices. If they want to they can alter the words to make it easier.

4. When they have managed to get some sort of beat into their spoken words, challenge them to match the word rhythms with their gesture rhythms, so that eventually the whole ask/refuse, demand/defend dialogue has a unified rhythm. Finally, ask them to round off the sequence by adding a bit in which the askers/demanders sulk away and do something to spite the refusers/defenders.

. Bring them back to the circle to discuss this, and ask if they have heard of the words 'nymph' and 'goblin'. Establish a nymph as a magic beautiful maiden who lived in rivers, the sea, hills or trees; and goblin as a mischievous, ugly demon. Give the children opportunities to try on the roles of nymph and goblin, reminding them of the contrasting movements you did at the beginning. Can they move from nymph into goblin, goblin into nymph?

6. Challenge them to rework their movements and words so that the askers/demanders are goblins and the refusers/defenders are nymphs. Can they keep the basics of their movement sequences whilst introducing these two roles?

Stage Two: Encountering the text

1. Without letting the children see the poem, read it to them, preferably on returning from the dance/drama lesson when their bodies and minds are tuned to its ideas. The words will then have experiences to match them.

2. Pin up the poster in a prominent position, then read it again, asking the children to follow it if they can. Repeat. Ask the children how nymphs and goblins would speak. What kinds of voices would they have? Establish key words such as high pitch/low pitch, shallow/deep, quiet/loud, quick/slow. Divide the class into nymphs and goblins and ask them to position themselves so that the nymphs are one side of the room, goblins the other. Ask the children to speak the poem in these positions, then let them swap roles and speak it again.

3. Give each child a copy and ask them to learn it by heart at home. At school consolidate this by running through the words each day. When the children know the words of the poem by heart, return to the hall and ask them to reconstruct the dance/drama sequences which they made at the start of the project. This time challenge them to add the words of Monro's poem to their work. Ask them to make any changes to their gestures which the words suggest.

4. Produce a performance of these encounters in which the nymphs enter, holding their beads and looking at them admiringly, then the goblins enter and approach their partner nymphs and begin the poem. Try to achieve an effect whereby all voices are in unison throughout.

Stage Three: Building on the text

̄ u ic

1. In the classroom re-explore the underlying rhythms in the poem by inviting the children to clap them out with long, strong claps (CLAP) and short, weak claps (clap). For instance, 'Nymph, nymph, what are your beads?' might go as follows 'CLAP, CLAP, clap-clap-clap, CLAP' and the reply, 'Green glass, goblin' 'CLAP, CLAP, clap-clap'. Once the children have got the hang of this, divide them into groups of two or three and allocate a few lines to each group. Arrange for them to demonstrate until the whole poem is covered by the clapping of the rhythm. Write it out on the blackboard in this sort of 'clap notation'.
2. Over a few days, each group working in turn, invite the children to match the claps with a small range of notes on chime bars and make this into a tune, allowing sufficient time. Try them out by arranging for one group to speak the poem while another group play their tune. Next, ask them to try and sing or chant the poem, using the tunes they have made. Ask them to write down the notes they used onto their copies of the poem. Share and record each one.
3. Discuss with the children the atmosphere of the poem. Apart from the voices of the nymph and the goblin, what other sounds might be heard? If this poem were in a film what kind of music or soundtrack would be playing in the background? Invite the groups to make a short soundtrack for the poem using the instruments available. The children should test the length of this piece by playing it with a reading of the text.
4. By now the children might have: (a) spoken poems, accompanied by tunes on chime bars; (b) sung versions of the poem; and (c) spoken poems, accompanied by atmospheric sound tracks. Let the groups try different mixes of these to create a finished piece of music.

Art

1. After the children have had plenty of the experiences suggested above, ask them each to do a series of drawings in sketchbooks of the nymph and goblin. Emphasise that they are creating ideas and it doesn't matter if the drawings are rough and ready. Ask them to imagine the place where they meet, the saltmarsh. What might be in its foreground and background? Ask them to make notes about this in the sketchbooks. With Reception and Year 1 pupils let them paint their pictures of the nymph and the goblin straight away
2. In order to enrich their art experiences in this work, particularly of the Year 2 children, try to obtain reproductions of seascapes, particularly of the margins: the

shores and the marshlands. An obvious source is the English artist J. M. W. Turner, but a number of French impressionists have produced interesting seascapes, worth investigating. You might also provide book illustrations of nymphs or fairies and goblins, but ensure that the children have fully developed their own images first. The fairy tale illustrations of Arthur Rackham, Michael Foreman and many others would be worth investigating. You might also introduce the children to the paintings of Hieronymous Bosch, Richard Dadd and other fantasy artists.

3. Give the children opportunities to find favourite images and copy them in their sketchbooks. Arrange group discussions to explore these further. Then ask the children to develop their own drawings further, taking in ideas which they have investigated.

4. This work can be developed in a variety of ways. The children could make individual portraits with seascape backgrounds and foregrounds. Or, collaborating with others, they might create a sequence of coloured drawings or paintings, which follows the poem. Or they could collaborate in the making of murals or friezes. Three dimensional models could be made and placed on marsh landscapes. They then become puppets and the poem could be spoken using them.

Writing

The poem offers opportunities for three kinds of creative writing: stories, playscripts and poems. What we have in the poem is an intriguing fragment of a story involving two characters, a goblin and a nymph. There are many questions posed by their brief encounter. What is so special about the beads? Why does the goblin want them so much? What sort of a creature will 'Lie in the mud and howl' for something?

1. Stories: Discuss this with the children and invite them to write the story *up to the moment of the meeting of nymph and goblin*. Invite them next to write the story of what happens next.

2. Playscripts: Teach the children that when you write characters' words in a script you write their name every time they speak, then write the words after it. Demonstrate this by writing out 'Overheard in a Saltmarsh' using this method, as follows:
Goblin. Nymph, nymph, what are your beads?
Nymph. Green glass, goblin. Why do you stare at them?
Goblin. Give them me.
Nymph. No.
Goblin. Give them me. Give them me.
Nymph. No.
Ask the children to imagine that the words in the poem were *only the ones that someone overheard on the saltmarsh* and that there were many more words exchanged between the nymph and the goblin. Invite them to extend the poem as a playscript backwards to when they first meet and forwards to when they part company.

3. Poems: Suggest to the children that they assume the role either of the nymph or the goblin. Ask them then to write vividly on: (a) the place where they live; (b) the

thoughts that they have after they have met; or (c) the treasures which they have in their hoards. Ask them to write as if they are Harold Monro on:

- the place on the moon where the beads were stolen from;
- the saltmarsh before they come; or
- the saltmarsh after they have gone.

4. Drafting: Arrange for the children to second draft their work by hand, share it with one another and mount a display alongside their visual art work. You might also invite them to word-process all the poems into an anthology and supply each of them with a copy. Arrange also for the playscripts to be performed, either with the dances and the musical pieces or as radio plays recorded onto tapes with sound effects and musical pieces.

Projects for Key Stage 2

Project 1: Exile

This project is particularly suitable for children who are studying the Anglo-Saxons in 'Raiders and settlers' in their history lessons.

Purpose: To develop poetry-writing
Length of time: One week

Focus: 'The Wanderer'[24]

> Extract 1
> "Often a lonely man longs for comfort,
> for his Maker's mercy when he's mournful
> and has to row the watery routes so long
> through icy seas, wading paths of exile:
> his destiny set." So said the wanderer,
> with miseries and gross murders in his mind,
> so many dearly loved kin put to death!
>
> "Often I am alone as each day breaks,
> mourning to myself, for no man is left
> living who I can unlock my heart to
> and talk openly. Too well do I know
> that noble custom among the great men
> to keep the heart's secrets closely guarded,
> locked inside the head, whatever is felt."
>
> Extract 2
> "Humbly I went on
> over the frozen waves, winter-saddened.
> Sullenly I sought a wealth-giver's hall,
> whether far or near, where I could find one
> who in that meadhall might understand me,
> bring solace to a solitary man

and treat me kindly. He who is tested
knows how sore a comrade sorrow can be
for one with few friends to care about him.
Exile is his gift, not the twisted gold,
a frozen body instead of earthly fame.
He remembers servants and precious gifts
and how when he was young his wondrous lord
treated him to feasts. Trashed is all this joy!"

Preparation

1. Work out and practise a mournful but strong way of reading the extract. It is important to get the pulsing rhythm right and to emphasise the alliteration in the poem. For instance, in the line 'for his *Maker's mer*cy when he's *mournful*' stress quite heavily the words in italics.

2. Make a glossary of the following words and teach them to the children before you start the work: 'Maker's' – God's; 'mournful' – sad; 'routes' – ways; 'exile' – being sent away from your country; 'destiny' – fate, what is in store for you; 'kin' – your family, including distant relatives; 'mourning' – when you're sad about the dead; 'noble' – high class, proud and fine; 'custom' – usual, the done thing; 'humbly' – obediently; 'sought' – looked for; 'solace' – comfort, sympathy; 'solitary' – alone; 'hall' and 'meadhall' – the place where a lord entertains his people, a very important place; 'comrade' – one who travels or works with you; 'earthly' – of this world. These words should be taken home and studied during the weekend before the project.

Drama

1. If possible, take the children to a desolate place: mountains, moorland, coast or forest. If not possible, use the school field. They will need to be suitably dressed and have a note-book which is easy to write in out of doors.

2. Tell the children that in Anglo-Saxon times one of the worst punishments would be to be sent into exile. This means that you could never be with your family and friends again. Often it might even mean you would have to be completely alone. Tell them also that a man could also be exiled if enemies attacked and killed his lord and all his family and friends.

3. Tell them that you have part of a poem about such an exiled man and read the two extracts of 'The Wanderer'. Ask the children to notice what a dreary, miserable life the wanderer has. What does he have to do? What has happened to him? What does he long for? Why can't he share his troubles? Have the children ever been in that situation of having problems and being unable to share them? Repeat the lines 'Exile is his gift not the twisted gold, a frozen body instead of earthly fame.' What exactly do they mean? What does the wanderer remember?

4. Tell the children that you and they are going to play a pretend game. If they are used to doing drama tell them you are all going to get *into role*, you as the Anglo-Saxon

lord, they as his kinsmen, who have committed crimes and are to be exiled. Each of them has to pretend that he or she is utterly alone and must not go near anyone else during this exile game.

5. The children must wander around the place writing exile poems, atempting to interpret the things they see as parts of their harsh situations.
6. Say to them that after re-reading each line of the extract you will exile one or two of them and proceed as follows: "'Often a lonely man longs for comfort'. Jenny and David. 'for his Maker's mercy when he's mournful. Tim and Gemma'" . . . . . and so on.

Redrafting

1. Back in the classroom ask the children to say briefly what things they saw and how they interpreted these things.
2. Ask the children if they are fully happy with what they have written or if they wish to improve it. For instance, they might be interested in building alliterative sounds into their lines or in replacing softer words with more rugged ones. The children might refer to the extracts for further inspiration in their redrafting. Have thesauruses available but don't overdo this. It is better not to change the material brought back to class too radically. You may be pleasantly surprised by the sound and tone of these poems even in the first draft. Here are some first draft examples from children who have enjoyed similar role-play writing games on this theme:

> The treacherous wind shortens my death.
> Love never occurred to me. I just keep going.
> Wearing a dark veil I see the water.
> Death follows shortly. (Philip)

> Wandering, wondering, weary.
> Once a warrior, now a lonely wanderer.
> Unwanted, unhappy he walks
> through his memories, alone. (Jane)

> I hear my master's death-call, I flee,
> Now to the end of time must I flee,
> flee from feasting halls.
> I am the bane of courage,
> Never can I be brave. (Neil)

> Walking in loneliness through zinc ruins,
> walking alone through bramble tripwires. (Clive)

Project 2: 'Tyger' and Visions

Purpose: To develop poetry-writing
Length: Three weeks

Focus i: Paintings by William Blake
Most of Blake's religious paintings are powerful and their clear, striking images, often of figures in adverse physical states, are ideal for generating imaginative response quickly for children in this age group. The majority of this work is in the Tate Gallery, London, and inexpensively available on postcards or posters. The aim for their use here is to prepare the children visually for their experience of 'Tyger'. Suggested pictures: Frontispiece of 'Visions of the Daughters of Albion', 'Satan smiting Job with sore Boils', 'The Simoniac Pope', 'The inscription over the Gate of Hell', 'Elohim creating Adam', the 'Urizen' collection, 'God judging Adam', 'Nebuchadnezzar', 'The Good and Evil Angels Struggling for Possession of a Child' and 'Hecate'.

Focus ii: 'Tyger'[11]

> Tyger! Tyger! burning bright
> In the forests of the night,
> What immortal hand or eye
> Could frame thy fearful symmetry?
>
> In what distant deeps or skies
> Burnt the fire of thine eyes?
> On what wings dare he aspire?
> What the hand dare seize the fire?
>
> And what shoulder, and what art
> Could twist the sinews of thy heart?
> And, when thy heart began to beat,
> What dread hand? and what dread feet?
>
> What the hammer? what the chain?
> In what furnace was thy brain?
> What the anvil? what dread grasp
> Dare its deadly terrors clasp?
>
> When the stars threw down their spears
> And water'd heaven with their tears
> Did he smile his work to see?
> Did he who made the lamb make thee?
>
> Tyger! Tyger! burning bright
> In the forests of the night
> What immortal hand or eye
> Dare frame thy fearful symmetry?

Stage One: Engaging with the pictures

1. Make a set of about twenty cards of Blake's paintings (as above) and allow the children to look through them. Ask them to choose one card that appeals strongly to them. This is better done in group work, but can be done in a class lesson if the children share.
2. Ask them to look long at the chosen card and to write lines about what they see. Emphasise that the idea is not to write a story. Ask them next to imagine the figures moving and to add more lines. These apparently simple requests may produce vivid lines such as these:

> Waves of the sea,
> a cauldron of deaths.
> Spirits almost swimming
> in a cave of evil.
> A firefooted man screaming.
> It's like the world
> burst into flames.
> The rocks and caves
> of this fiery world
> are almost telling,
> telling a story of death.

Simply by interpreting the strange images in Blake's paintings literally the children will make two gains: (a) expand their consciousness by exploring such unusual imagery; and (b) adopt a style suitable for writing imaginatively. This will benefit them when they write in response to 'Tyger'. You will find that almost every child will be able to create lines of poetry, by which I mean in this context, lines of original perception expressed in a memorable way.

3. Allow the children to repeat this with other cards.

Stage Two: Engaging with 'Tyger'

Before any further work is done the children should learn the poem and spend time chanting it in various ways and with various combinations of voices.

1. Movement:
   - Adopt the same pattern for the movement lesson as decribed in the Key Stage 1 'Day, night and dreams' project: Warming up; working on the poem; calming down. For warm ups ask the children to move with tigerlike strides chanting the poem. This can be varied by making hammering metal movements and throwing movements for later in the poem.
   - Continue the idea of interpreting what Blake creates literally. For instance, discuss the notion of 'fearful symmetry', which should lead to the idea of a symmetrical pattern which is frightening. Interpret this in movement by asking the children to make *tableaux vivants* (living pictures) in groups which are terrifying! They will have much to draw on having worked with the Blake paintings.

- Use the *tableaux vivants* approach to make all the key pictures in the poem. Say to the children that they are like videos with the pause button on. This should then lead to the *tableaux* unfreezing into movements, again, to the rhythm of the chanted poem.
- If time allows ask the children to use percussion instruments and make variations to the basic rhythm of the poem. They should compose simple pieces to accompany their movements and the chanting.

2. Writing:

- William Blake's interest in 'Tyger' is not to describe the tiger but to speculate about its making. He asks many questions and, thereby, provides rich openings for children to write in a kind of answering mode.
- The following are the key openings for writing to set your children:

  a) Imagine you are in the 'forests of the night'. You see Tyger but he doesn't see you or harm you. Write your own poem about what you see.

  b) According to Blake's poem, Tyger was made somewhere else out of different things, but Blake doesn't know where or what. Imagine the making of Tyger. Write your poem about that.

  c) How can stars throw spears and shed tears? They must be strange stars! Write your poem about such stars.

  d) Imagine that 'immortal hand' and 'immortal eye' and the immortal being that they are part of. 'Did he smile his work to see?' Write your poem about this immortal being who created Tyger.

If this work is successful – and time allows – let the children paint. Organise a sharing of this work to other classes in the school: the dance, the poems and the painting.

Project 3: 'Inversnaid'

Purpose: To develop response across the arts
Length: Six weeks or half a term

Focus: 'Inversnaid'[26]

> This darksome burn, horseback brown,
> His rollrock highroad roaring down,
> In coop and in comb the fleece of his foam
> Flutes and low to the lake falls home.
>
> A windpuff-bonnet of fawn-froth
> Turns and twindles over the broth
> Of a pool so pitchblack, fell frowning,
> It rounds and rounds despair to drowning.
>
> Degged with dew, dappled with dew
> Are the groins of the braes that the brook treads through,
> Wiry heathpacks, flitches of fern,
> And the beadbonny ash that sits over the burn.

What would the world be, once bereft
Of wet and of wildness? Let them be left,
O let them be left, wildness and wet;
Long live the weeds and the wilderness yet.

Preparation

1. Make a large poster copy and individual copies of Hopkins' poem.
2. Practise reading the poem so that you develop your best possible performance for the children. Pay particular attention to where you place the emphasis of your voice, how you can vary the volume and pace, how you can convey the sense of a fast-flowing stream.

Stage One: Engaging with the text by conferencing

1. After reading the poem to the children, give each child a copy. Divide the class into small groups and ask them simply to try and work the poem out following the suggestions for conferencing in Chapter Four. Provide dictionaries or, to speed up the flow of ideas, provide the children with the following glossary:
   burn = stream, coop = confined space, place where chickens are kept,
   bonnet = girl's or woman's hat in the olden days, fawn = pale brown,
   twindles = twists and dwindles, fell = mountain, aggressive,
   despair = a feeling of complete hopelessness, degged = speckled,
   groins = where the legs join the body, lines of posts on beaches,
   braes = small valleys, flitches = sides of pork, bonny = plump and pretty,
   bereft = utterly lost
2. Ask the children to write their ideas, ready to present to the whole class. Encourage diverse views as well as consensual ones. As you move around the groups, keep drawing the children's attention to the key images in the poem and what Hopkins might have had in mind.
3. Allow your plenary session sufficient time for the full development of ideas, then attempt to sum up the key ones and add any ideas you have, which were not raised by the groups.
4. Ask the groups to write their ideas in full on the computer, then gather them together in a folder, which is readily available for everybody to read.
5. Conclude this stage of the work by asking the children to take away their copies of the poem and learn it by heart. Hold a short 'Inversnaid'-learning session each day during this period to consolidate the work at home.

Stage Two: Getting the text in the air

1. Give every child the opportunity of speaking the poem out loud without the script and with you as prompt. This should be done in groups to avoid putting too much pressure on individuals. However, children are fully capable of learning this poem and should be expected to do so.

2. The children, particularly if they are Year 5 or Year 6 pupils, are also fully capable of accommodating some knowledge of the formal aspects of 'Inversnaid' at this stage of the project. So ask the groups to conference again, this time focusing on the form of the poem. Allocate a different task to each group as follows:

   Group 1. Rhyme scheme: Find the pairs of rhyming words. What is the pattern and what effect does this have on the rhythm of the poem?

   Group 2. Alliteration: Alliteration is when words begin with the same sound. Find the alliterating letters in each verse of the poem. What kinds of sounds are these, hard or soft or a mixture of both? What effect does this have on the rhythm of the poem?

   Group 3. Imagery: Metaphors are when one thing is made into something else, such as the stream being called a 'highroad'. Find as many metaphors as you can. What do they add to the picture which the poet creates?

   Group 4. The poem's overall message: Hopkins communicates a very strong message in this poem, which seems to be trying to persuade us to do something. What is his message? How does he try to make us take notice of it? Look at the whole poem and try to work out how well Hopkins makes his argument.

3. Ask the groups to write down their observations and opinions, then present them to one another. Emphasise the importance of practising this and speaking clearly. Each group should work also on speaking the poem out loud, without using scripts. Challenge them to use interesting ways of combining their voices. Allow an open discussion after each presentation and add your own observations at this stage.

4. Ask the groups to write their ideas in full on the computer and to gather them together for others to read.

Stage Three: Expressive engagement through visual art

1. A close focus on the images of the poem should also be the main feature of the children's expressive engagement through visual art. Having pursued meaning in image in their conferences the children will be powerfully influenced in visual terms.

2. Although some of the impulses provoked by Hopkins' ideas and images may not be fully realised in the children's final forms because of their lack of technique, the intent behind them is what is important.

3. At this point it needs to be emphasised that an exploratory, responsive and creative ambience needs to be developed, particularly in this expressive work. It will prove crucial to the children's depth of response.

4. Ask each child to focus on a key image in the poem such as the 'horseback brown/rollrock highroad' image or 'coop and comb/fleece of his foam'. When they have settled on an image invite them to do a series of drawings to represent what they see, then ask them to decide what media they wish to use. Depending on what is available and how experienced they are, allow them an open-ended choice.

5. Here are descriptions of some memorable examples of children's work done on a pilot project based on this poem:

a) Barbara wanted to represent the spiralling ideas in 'turns and twindles' and 'rounds and rounds'. She wanted a sense of depth, of three dimensions and couldn't work out how to create it until she remembered doing cut-out Christmas decorations. She spent a great deal of time getting her cuts right so as to produce the contrast between turn, twindle and round. The finished piece has two of these spirals, painted, and attached to a background of a brackish-coloured flowing river.

b) Michael was attracted to the ideas arising out of the word comb, which he read as meaning the shapes of rocks in the river being like a comb to pull through hair. He painted a river and made a series of long, rocklike points from card, which He painted. He then made slits in the picture and pushed the points in through them from the back.

c) Kim had the surreal notion of a brown horse galloping, its tail at full stretch behind it. This tail is the source of the river, which flows wildly from it. It was attempted in paint and Kim tried to represent the various movements in the poem in patterns.

d) Lee was interested in the idea of what things look like behind water. He wanted to show the horse image as an actual horse behind water. He spent time looking at different things behind running tapwater then tried to get that effect in a painting of a horse behind a river.

Stage Four: Expressive engagement through dance

1. In your P.E. lessons get the children to explore key ideas in the poem in movement. By now the children will have very clear pictures of the complexities in the imagery. So direct them, for instance, to galloping horse movements, the rock shapes implied by 'coop and comb' and the movement differences implied in phrases such as 'turns and twindles'. Valuable insights can also be obtained using the *tableaux vivants* approach on images such as 'beadbonny ash'. These exercises should provide a sort of basic course before the children are invited to form groups to explore the movement possibilities of the poem in a dance drama.

2. Allow the pupils to choreograph and rehearse their own pieces and save your contribution for coaching the actual quality definition of each shape and movement they produce. Choose a piece of suitable recorded music to add atmosphere to the work.

3. As accurately as I can convey the movements in words, here is a description of a dance, in six phases, which was done on the pilot for this poem:

Phase A: the stream bubbles out of the moors. The dancers are lying in a circle head to toe. Each dancer jerks a different part of her body sluggishly to make a slow, bubbly effect. This is weak and recedes, but reasserts itself.

Phase B: it trickles down. The dancers stretch high in the circle, arms raised then down and crossed in front of them, one after the other – follow the leader style, creating a waviness.

Phase C: it 'twindles', moves in and out of the rocks. Every alternate dancer moves to centre circle leaving the others on the circumference. The centre group makes a star-patterned comb with upward points. The dancers on the circumference then rush between each tooth of it.

Phase D: it whirls. The dancers divide into two groups making various twisting, twindling, cooping and combing sequences, as follows:

i.   the first group makes a linear pattern going down, rolling over, one after the other with heads tossing like horses to show off manes, then getting cooped up and into comb shapes;

ii.   the second group twists, then two dancers come together in the centre, push hands together, across, rejoin, hold, gather a third dancer, then a fourth, repeat. The fifth is trapped in a coop and is unable to join the others;

iii. the second group makes a whole-group comb shape and the first group twists in and out of it, whirls round the outside, followed by the second group and all move into a spiral.

Phase E: it becomes a waterfall. This large spiral becomes a waterfall in a new place in the hall. It is caused by one dancer twisting off the others, away and falling flat to the ground. The others follow in low and middle spread and twisting shapes and gather around and above the first dancer.

Phase F: it falls 'home' to the lake. The dancers return to their circle, but this time it is whirling and twisting as if at the bottom of a whirlpool. They close and fall into a still, flat, whole-group shape: the lake.

This dance was composed and choreographed collaboratively by the children after they had visited a real river – the River Conwy – from source to estuary, as part of their river project in Geography.

Stage Five: Expressive engagement through writing

1. Organise a visit to a river, following it from source to estuary, if possible, and making key stops along the way. As well as providing Geographical tasks for the children to do, add poetry-writing tasks. You might give them four: the mountain stream; the waterfalls or rapids; the river meandering; and the estuary.

2. The children's work will be from direct, first-hand experience of the river but will be influenced by all their previous experiences in this project. The children's poems will show a positive 'Hopkins influence'. This will be found in the imagery which they use. Images of froth and foam (as in 'the fleece of his foam' and 'windpuff bonnet of fawn froth') may be common in many children's work.

3. Evidence of the internalisation of Hopkins' theme and form may be revealed by the different applications of it to what individual children experience on the visit. At the simplest level of engagement with the Hopkins image a child may merely see froth in the stream and use it in the composition, as in 'Through the foam there is a rush of water' from the pilot project. However, at a deeper level the child may be able to take possession of the metaphor and make it new as in 'a bride's trailing veil'. This is a growth out of the 'windpuff bonnet' metaphor for froth. The child has internalised

Hopkins' bonnet metaphor during the previous weeks of playing and has recast it in a metaphor which is new but of the same species as the original.

4. Arrange for the children to second draft their work by hand, share it with one another and mount a display alongside their visual art work. You might also invite them to word-process all their poems into an anthology and supply each of them with a copy.

References

1. Heard in a poetry reading by Michael Horovitz in Wrexham Library Arts Centre, 1990.
2. Gaston Bachelard (1969) *The Poetics of Reverie*, Beacon Press, Boston, USA.
3. Corbett, P. and Moses, B. (1986), *Catapults and Kingfishers*, OUP, Oxford.
4. Bachelard (1969) *The Poetics of Reverie*, Beacon Press, Boston, USA.
5. Ibid.
6. Ibid.
7. Ibid.
8. Ibid.
9. Keats. J. 'La Belle Dame Sans Merci' in (1955) *The Poems of John Keats*, Collins, London.
10. Mallarme, S. 'Sonnet (For your dear dead one, her friend)' (1977) *The Poems*, Penguin, Harmondsworth.
11. Blake, W. 'Tyger' in (1927) *Poems and Prophecies*, Dent, London.
12. Mandelstam, O. 'Stone 24' in (1973) *Selected Poems*, OUP, Oxford.
13. Fitzgerald, R. (1961) *The Odyssey*, Collins Harvill, London.
14. Holub, M. 'At last' in (1997), *The Rampage*, Faber, London.
15. Hughes, T. 'Wind' in (1957) *The Hawk in the Rain*, Faber, London.
16. Bachelard (1969) *The Poetics of Reverie*, Beacon Press, Boston, USA
17. Pope, A. 'The Rape of the Lock' in (1924) *Poems*, Dent, London.
18. Eliot, T.S. 'Introduction' to (1928) Pound, E. *Selected Poems*, Faber, London.
19. Holub. M. 'The Door', in (1967) *Selected Poems*, Penguin, Harmonsworth.
20. de la Mare, W. 'Hide and Seek' in (1944) *Collected Rhymes and Verses*, Faber, London.
21. Stevenson, R.L. 'Windy Nights', in (1953) *The Faber Book of Children's Verse*, Faber, London.
22. Causley, C. 'Dream Poem', in *Collected Poems*, Macmillan, London.
23. Monro, H. 'Overheard on a Saltmarsh' in (1933) *Collected Poems*, Duckworth, London.
24. Unpublished translation by Dennis Carter from Leslie, R. F. (Ed.) (1966) *Three Old English Elegies*, Manchester University Press, Manchester.
25. Hopkins, G.M. 'Inversnaid' in (1953) Gardner, W.H. (Ed.) *Gerard Manley Hopkins: A Selection of his Poems and Prose*, Penguin, Harmondsworth.

Chapter Six

Interpretations of the Material World

Poets transforming the world

In his collection of poems *Seeing Things*, Seamus Heaney explores the link between the ordinary and the marvellous. For Heaney the marvellous is actually present in ordinary everyday objects, people, places and experiences. He finds revelations of the marvellous in such common objects as a pitchfork, an old picture, a bicycle wheel going round quickly and an old bed. Similarly, a game of football when he was a boy, using coats as goalposts, is transformed by memory into a visionary moment in which 'Some time limit had been passed . . . . .' In another of these poems, 'Fosterling', he writes that he had to wait until he 'was nearly fifty To credit marvels'. For Heaney, doing this appears to be something which adults need to work at.[1]

This is a feeling common to many poets and philosophers. William Wordsworth, along with many poets of the Romantic period in European poetry, believed that this ability 'to credit marvels' is naturally present in children, but is lost once we grow into adulthood. Wordsworth's famous 'Ode on Intimations of Immortality'[2] is partly based on his sense of losing this ability. Philosophers such as Theodore Roszak, the American, claim that the ability to see that 'everything is simultaneously ordinary and sacred' is present in all of us so long as we maintain the eyes to see it.[3]

Children and the world

I dwell on this idea here because I believe that the ability 'to credit marvels' is essential for the reading and making of poetry, almost all of which occurs in the area where the ordinary and extraordinary are linked. Children already have this ability before we try to teach them anything in school; so they will respond to poetry, and make it in lessons, if we help their natural ability to have outlets. One only has to spend time listening to three-year-olds to realise just how well developed this ability is. For instance, here is a sequence of sayings of a child starting a month before his fourth birthday:

- The child returns from visiting the nursery school he will soon attend and laughs when his mum tells his dad about the Headteacher. 'She's the one who teaches your head!' he exclaims.

- Three days later he is in the garden in the early morning and notices his long shadow and says, laughing 'I've grown bigger. May I have wine now?'
- Later that month he plays with Duplo bricks and drops a few. It annoys him and he snaps, 'I've got stupid hands today. I wish I was an octopus.'
- Sitting on the toilet, he says, 'When I'm poohing, it's like a butterfly opening.'
- He has had many experiences with books, handling them, having them read to him, developing a knowledge of how they are structured and the worlds they access, but he cannot yet read properly. One day he says to his big brother, 'Hey, can I have a chapter of tickling?'
- It's three days before his fourth birthday and he's just been down the new chute in the local leisure pool. He is excited about this experience and says, 'It's like a door opening and squashing you flat and afterwards you puff again like in the cartoons.'

Now, in terms of his real life these are ordinary experiences. He visits his new school, watches his shadow, plays with toys, goes to the toilet, plays with his big brother, and goes to the baths. These are typical childhood pursuits for millions of children throughout the world. What makes them interesting here is the way that the child's perception, in reporting them, transforms them into something special, something particular. An important attendant feature is the presence of responsive listeners, whom he expects to be interested. There are important lessons for teachers in this.

In terms of the formalities of poetry, the child's sayings are particularly interesting for their deployment of imagery. They are metaphorically adventurous and witty. If we think of metaphor as one of poetry's equations, he equates various strands of his experiences. So, opening anus = butterfly opening wings; landing in water = transformations of cartoon characters. It is the particular way that these metaphors emerge naturally, and quite subtly and wittily, which makes them memorable. However, the purpose of quoting them here is to locate poetry where it really begins: in the human attempt to make sense of a world which often appears fragmentary to us. This child, robustly alive in the world, is delighted to create these little unities. An equation, whether in mathematics or in poetry, is the discovery of unity, of coherence, of meaning in the vast, often confusing world we all share.

If this inborn ability in young children gives each of them what Heaney, referring to John Clare's poetic voice, has called an 'unmistakable signature', then there are implications here for a different kind of pedagogy. Certain current practises in the teaching of poetry-writing militate strongly against the development of each child's 'unmistakable signature'.[4] One instance is the practise of making a blackboard focus for the whole class on the same object, which often begins with a so-called class discussion and a list of words and phrases being compiled. Then the children are expected to write their own poems. But the whole experience, however well planned, is controlled by the teacher, the children's openings strictly limited as they are caught within someone else's agenda. The children will give back what they think is expected of them. There is little space, in this pedagogy, for innovation, for the kind of insight revealed in the child's natural utterances quoted above. They cannot engage in reverie, in this stiff framework of demands. This is not to deny the difficulty of 'getting some children started' in the writing of poetry. However, there are pedagogies available which do not go against the grain of children's individual response, some of which are offered in this book.

Developing response to the world

Perhaps we cannot actually teach children to write poetically at all. The more we teach about form and practise the further we may move away from these kinds of 'signatures' in the voices of the children. Instead, we should think about the creation of a 'poetic environment' which will encourage the development of expressive signatures. The poetic environment I have in mind involves all manner of objects both inside and outside the classroom. It involves the pupils in being 'on the look-out' for poems outside of lessons, being aware that there are poems all around, waiting to be written. In an environment of this sort pupils have plans and lessons set up by the teacher, but are involved in setting their own agendas. Even if there is only an hour a week, or less, available for such an approach, this can be achieved.

As discussed in Chapter One, such a poetic environment crucially depends upon an adventurous use of language, within which jokes, word games, punning, the bizarre and the ludicrous have a place as part of everyday classroom interactions in language. The teacher will not only encourage her children to be adventurous with words, and to share their perceptions outside of school, but will also contribute to the adventure from her own stock of words and perceptions. Part of the adventure with language will also involve the 'study' of language forms, the derivations of words, place-names, surnames and slang.

This sense of the excitement and richness in words themselves should be present in most parts of the curriculum. For instance, the classroom ought not only to have its dictionaries and thesauruses, but also its dictionaries of English Place-Names, Idioms, Proverbs and many others besides. When studying maps as part of history or geography lessons the names of features, towns and villages will be interesting in their own right, not merely to denote points on the map. For instance, one day a group of children, pondering the possible meaning of a strange village name such as 'Shocklach' in Cheshire, might discover the amazing truth that it means 'goblin-stream', and be sparked to speculate about the story behind that.[5]

What needs to be avoided in this focus on words themselves is too heavy an insistence on their existence as labels when the truths and stories *behind* words can be seen as inspirational. So, we may teach children that 'to charge' is a verb and that 'charge' is a noun, but the teacher in the poetic environment I am describing will also be keen to point to the fact that these words were brought to our language by the Normans with the word *charger*. The children may be fascinated to explore the many variations in the word's meanings, from a knight on horseback (lance in hand, making for his opponent) to the filling up of a ship with cargoes, to how much something costs in a shop, to the amount of electricity in a battery. Older children can be shown that these meanings actually grew around the word and were not fixed. Given the opportunity, some might discover when different meanings for the word are first recorded. Thus they will see that words, like towns, are built over the centuries.

This kind of 'knowledge about language' is a far cry from the kind of 'understanding' envisaged in post-Dearing English lessons and implicit in this statement from the Programmes of Study for English at Key Stage 1:

> They (pupils) should be taught to use their knowledge about language gained from reading, to develop their understanding of standard English.[6]

A proper concern for words and for primary children's growing powers in using them will recognise the evocative nature of language as well as its literal meanings. Such a concern will recognise and value the mental pictures that one word may trigger. Thus 'charge' may show us two stags in spring running at each other and cracking their skulls together. On the other hand, it may show a Visa card being handed across a counter.

The word's power to evoke will concern the teacher working to provide a poetic environment for her children. One day such a concern just might lead to a deep and dynamic revelation for an individual reading these lines of Gerard Manley Hopkins's sonnet 'God's Grandeur'[7]:

> **The world is charged with the grandeur of God.**
> **It will flame out, like shining from shook foil;**
> **It gathers to a greatness, like the ooze of oil**
> **Crushed.**

Here we have the stunning ambiguity that the word 'charge' has now acquired. The word itself has been 'charged' with an extraordinary power of meaning. On the one hand, it is heavy; it is loaded. On the other, it is light and quick; it sizzles and shines. Such perceptions of the evocative power of one word may open up a reader's sense of a poet's whole reverie, the metaphorical world he has created. Such perceptions are a form of wisdom. But they are not gained from the dreary grind through grammar exercises, which seem to be such a widespread development in post-1988 schools' English.

The kind of attitudes, provisions and practises which I have described in this section can lead to poems such as this, written by ten-year-old David one autumn:

> **'Weather'**
> **Wind blasts leaves in your pathway.**
> **Frost chokes the boughs and makes**
> **them release their jewels.**
> **Rain bursts from the clouds and hisses**
> **at the leaves when it hits them.**
> **The winter begins to show**
> **and chills the earth. It becomes a crust**
> **with a soft underneath like bread.**

Here autumn is dramatically powerful. It 'blasts', it 'chokes' and it 'bursts', yet somehow it is also benign and homely. It brings us 'jewels' and it brings us 'bread'. The child's reverie towards autumn may be slightly frightening, with the hint of hissing snakes among the leaves, but it is also a place where the child belongs.

The journey from the three-year-old's talk about himself, the people he meets and his experiences, to this self-assured poem which explores a well-known season so simply and so sensuously, is not very far at all. There is the same relationship between the child and the world, at work and at play. There is the same delight in exploring it and making from it. Here is a continuum for a nourishing, life-enhancing way of 'seeing things', which can be maintained throughout the primary school in the kind of context in which teachers enable children to 'credit marvels' in their ordinary worlds, just as this child has done in his autumn poem. Teachers will, of course, also need to take direct measures to re-establish this context for those pupils who appear to have temporarily mislaid such a relationship with the world.

The poetic environment includes the voices of well-known poets, past and present. Their songs are exchanged and played with in all sorts of ways. Some of the most memorable songs, or extracts of them, are memorised and become part of the child's cadence; and sometimes pupils imitate models provided by the great singers, but not slavishly and without the stifling effect of too much reverence being shown. In the poetic environment I am suggesting, the child will, as it were, dream or play along with the poet. This will involve a reverie in the reading; which is similar to a reverie which may lead into writing.

Through this approach children will have ready and easy access to a whole body of poetry, including the poems of past pupils in the school. They will also be involved in the kinds of activity presented throughout this book. Over time a body of work may accumulate in a school which is fed from many cultures of the world and from many generations of the school, to become a strong and rich resource, a source of pleasure, instruction, of models and encouragements. This is the very essence of culture.

Using poets' work

Most children's experiences of the world outside them, both at home and at school, will tend to be interpreted by those they share it with in a prosaic way. Adults assume the responsibility of preparing the young for survival in the world according to the expectations that any society projects upon its people. Except in earlier societies, in which the power of dreaming and ritual were fundamental to survival, the development of an imaginative engagement with the material world is not part of the agenda. This is understandable. Most of us wish to care for our children and desire, as it were, to release them into the world as young adults who will be successful.

However, I would argue that the most basic requirements for all round success in the world are respect for oneself and respect for the world or, to put it more strongly, love of oneself and love of the world. In Chapter Five of this book I describe ways of developing children's reverie and imagination and I would claim that such activity generates the healthy kind of respect or love for oneself which I have in mind. I hope I have demonstrated the fundamental role that the poets can have in such developments. Here, in Chapter Six, I am attempting to argue that, through the transformative application of children's imaginations onto external reality, they may develop respect and love for the world which they share with everyone else.

What I am saying is that the teaching of poetry in the primary school should not be an end in itself nor merely a means to the end of developing the literacy of the children. There should be this much greater ambition which is to do with the way we value or do not value life itself. I am arguing that the young child's natural tendency to turn the ordinary into the extraordinary is a manifestation of that child's self respect and love and a respect and love for the world. Such powers as these – and 'powers' is the only word to use – have to be maintained and the poetic way of seeing and of using language has, as it were, many tools for the job.

However, the use of poets' work in the process of maintaining the child's transformative way of seeing the world has to be handled carefully. It should be used to assist children's natural developments rather than replacing them. It should present options rather than rules. For this reason metaphor is of great value to children because it extends a way of making sense of the world that children already operate naturally. Similarly, a rhythmic use of language matches the exuberant way that children move and think and speak.

The reality of all this inside a classroom is best illustrated by imagining what might be in a display that a teacher might prepare for her class. Let us imagine that the teacher has planned to do cross-curricular work on spring immediately after the children return from the Easter holidays. This might have started with the programme of study for science, 'Life processes and living things', which is in the school's planning for this particular term. However, the teacher wishes to engage the children imaginatively with the theme and to make an impact with a display. So, perhaps she mounts a reproduction of a painting of spring trees by Cézanne[8] and the more scientific drawings of plants by Leonardo[9]. She picks some twigs of a number of different species of tree and arranges them in different vases.

The display of objects builds up and words need to be added to it. Now, in most classrooms, the teacher's use of the written word consists of name labels and extracts of information as in a museum and this has the effect of consolidating a factual, prosaic way of seeing life processes and living things. But, let us say that our teacher were to pin up these two lines from Edith Sitwell's 'Bucolic Comedies' next to the spring twigs, 'The trees were hissing like green geese/The words they tried to say were these'?[10] The inclusion of these lines would immediately open the door to an entirely different kind of engagement with trees. The teacher could use these two lines as a means to involve the children in a reverie about what trees might think and feel. She might take her class for a short spring walk with the question 'What words might these trees be trying to say?'

Simply by using Sitwell's lines the teacher has widened the entire scope of her project, introducing into it the potential for the children to empathise with trees. The same could be done for the children's attitudes towards wild flowers by the inclusion of Hopkins's memorable line about spring, 'when weeds in wheels shoot long and lovely and lush'[11] or for their notions about small creatures by Philip Gross's lines about snails, 'They lift small frills/to glide and teeter, balancing their shells/like the family china.'[12]

Such lines of poetry, as it were, bless weeds and snails, bestowing greater value on them. They also might validate the imaginative curiosity of the children.

As this 'life processes and living things' project proceeds, the teacher may continue to develop the children's poetic as well as their scientific relationship with the natural world. Depending on the age of the children, they might engage with nature poems by John Clare, Andrew Young, Edward Thomas, Wordsworth and Ted Hughes. They will also write their own, like this acute observation and profound imagination of the sound a blackbird makes underneath a hedge, written by Simon:

> Scurry sound,
> scuffles around the leaves
> like the peck of a bird's beak
> sounding around the worm's ear,
> bellowing, pecking,
> peck, peck, peck got him!
> The worm's ears ring no more.

In this poem the child transforms the observation of an everyday sound into the nightmare experienced by a lowly worm. Such a poem has all the power of myth as do many of the nature poems of Ted Hughes and Seamus Heaney. It is by the inclusion of such work to complement children's classroom experiences that the agenda of possibilities can always be kept open for a more visionary relationship with the material world as well as for a factual and scientific relationship. Ultimately, the two are mutually *inclusive*. The three projects which follow are attempts to provide models for this.

Projects for Key Stages 1 and 2

Project 1: Keepsakes

Purpose: To develop poetry-writing
Length of time: One week

Focus i: Objects brought in by the children
Focus ii. 'the african pot'[13]

> it is round and fat and squat
> it has no handle and the rim has no spout
> at first it seems as if the colours have
> no co-ordination and no rhythm
> the yellow and brown stripes circle
> the pot in quick diagonals
>
> i puzzle over the absence of the handle
> and then suddenly i think of a young woman
> wearing beads walking to a river with
> the pot gracefully balanced on her head

and then the colours begin the rhyme
yellow zigzagging around the top
makes me think of harvest time of golden corn
of dances around an autumn fire of ripe fruit
and of men drinking homebrewed beer

and as i stroke the brown
i can almost feel the full earth between
my fingers earth that echoes the thunderous
stamp of warriors going to war earth that
offers base accompaniment to dancing feet
i can almost see an ox pulling a plough
steered by a man of infinite patience
making ordered rows of upturned loam

the maker made this pot
with a song in his heart
and a vision in his eyes
lifting it up i can almost hear
him say
   i am man
   life is but clay in my hands
   creation is at my fingertips

Focus iii: 'The old pair of bellows'

I have a wooden beech overcoat
and a leather lining.
My iron snout grovels in
the burning coals and embers.
My studded forehead
protects my leather skin.
(Andrew McMorran, age 11)

Experiencing the keepsakes

1. Ask the children to bring in an object from home which has sentimental or other importance to their whole family. Suggest that it should not be a toy. (There are suggestions for work on toys in Chapter Five of this book.) Rather, it should be something that has a different kind of significance and value. If any child cannot bring in the actual object because it is too valuable, ask them to spend some time looking at it, feeling it and finding out about it from their family.

2. When they have brought in their objects, or information about them, allow each child to share with the whole class. Tell the children they will be writing about the objects later. First of all they will look at a poem about another precious object.

Experiencing 'the african pot'

1. Read Johennese's 'the african pot' to the class and tell them it is about an object made by a potter in an African village.
2. Ask the children to read the poem a line each in register order and to try and make it flow. Keep going until the poem has been read about three times.
3. Divide the class into five discussion groups and allocate a verse to each group and ask the groups the following two questions:
   a) What is so special about the object?
   b) What do you think your verse is saying about the pot?
4. Hold a plenary session and ask the groups to present their ideas.
5. Talk to the children about the poet's way of writing about the pot:
   a) He describes it – 'it is round and fat and squat'.
   b) He wonders about it because it has some mystery attached to it – ' i puzzle'.
   c) Then he realises the answer to the mystery – 'then suddenly i think of harvest time'.
   d) By 'stroking' the pot he remembers lots of other things about it. It is almost like Aladdin's lamp but instead of a geni it is many interesting happenings that are recalled.
   e) He thinks of the 'maker' of the pot and imagines what he was like when he made it.
6. This offers a useful structure for older children to use: describe – wonder about – answer – recall – imagine its maker.

Preparing for writing

1. So, with older children use this poem as a good model, but don't make it into a rigid formula for their own poetry-writing.
2. With younger children use the bellows poem. Tell them that bellows were used for getting a fire going but are not used very often now. Tell them that they were made out of beechwood, leather, iron and other metals.
3. Read the poem to the children and establish that the poet (a Year 6 child called Andrew) calls the wooden sides an 'overcoat', the iron part that goes in the fire a 'snout' (nose), the studs attaching the leather to the wood, a 'forehead' and the leather itself a 'skin'. In other words he compares the bellows to some sort of person by using metaphors. Try to establish this as a way of writing about their own objects, by using some metaphors.

Writing poems about keepsakes

1. Ask the children to look at their objects or think about them if they are at home. Try to get them really meditating. When they are engaging with their objects as you want them to ask them to write their poems.
2. If you feel that a more gradual or structured approach is required, try the following, using these words.

a) Write the object's name.

b) Describe it, using any poetic devices can manage, e.g. simile, metaphor or other comparison.

c) *EITHER* imagine where it came from or might have come from. See the place and try to write about it vividly. *OR* if there is something unknown or mysterious about the object, speculate about it. Imagine an answer for its mystery and write that.

d) Feel the object and try to remember more things about it. Write them.

e) *EITHER* think of other things it reminds you of and make metaphors out of them. OR imagine who made it and write about that maker.

6. Redraft work, if necessary, and share.

7. Set up a 'keepsakes' display. If possible, include some of the objects in the display. When the display comes down make a book for the poems and any illustrations which are done.

Project 2: Autumn shone forth (KS 1 and 2)

Purpose: To develop poetry-writing
Length: Three weeks

Week One Focus: Four haiku from ancient Japan.[14]

> Pitiful, afraid
> the poor scarecrows look like men
> in autumn moonlight. (Shiki)

> September sunshine –
> the hovering dragonfly's
> shimmering shadow. (Karo)

> Exquisite the dewy
> bramble – to every thorn
> a single droplet. (Buson)

> Nights are getting cold –
> not a single insect now
> attacks the candle. (Shiki)

Experiencing the haiku

1. These short poems usually have about seventeen syllables or beats altogether, with five on the first line, seven on the second and five on the third. The Japanese poets who wrote them looked very closely at the world in which they lived. They looked for little examples of what was going on. For instance, the fact that hardly any insects come to a candle shows the change in the season of the year. Tell the children these basic facts about the haiku before reading them.

2. Read the haiku to the class in a soft but clear voice. Ask the children in pairs to read one of the haiku out loud to each other and to discuss which is the best way to say it. They should then try to learn their chosen haiku, as quickly as possible so that they can speak it in the right voice without looking at it.

3. Each haiku contains a clear picture and to 'get' the poem you have clearly to see that picture. The pairs of children to tell each other exactly what they see when they hear the poem and to write this down.

4. Ask for volunteers to read each of the four haiku to the class and others to say what they see when they hear them.

5. Ask the children also to say to their partners what they feel when they hear the haiku. Repeat readings of the haiku with different children saying what the words make them feel. Ask them to write this down also.

6. If time allows, the children to do water colour paintings of what the haiku make them see.

Writing haiku

1. The seventeen syllables rule is only rough and ready, but it is a helpful guide for beginners and is well worth setting as a rule.

2. During the weekend prior to the haiku week ask the children to look for little signs of autumn or objects which are autumnal and to bring them to school on the Monday. Bring plenty of things yourself for those who come empty-handed.

3. Before asking the children to write, get some of them to say the four haiku again to create the right mood. Remind them of the seventeen syllable rule, then ask them to have a go without fear of failure.

4. Encourage the children to have plenty of attempts at the form until each of them has at least one haiku to be proud of.

5. Allow time for redrafting and sharing. Make a class book for autumn poems and ask the children to illustrate their work.

Week Two Focus: 'Beech Tree'[15]

> *The January tree*
> *all lost and forlorn*
> *is the poorest and coldest*
> *tree of them all.*

> Spendthrift October beech
> showers gold
> and copper coins to wind
> blowing cold
> lets fall his encased gems
> to the mould,
> deserted by the sun
> growing old.

But the January tree
all lost and forlorn
is the poorest and coldest
tree of them all.

Bankrupt November beech
soon beholds
branches fretted bare by
north wind's scolds.
Pauper December beech
rare sap holds
tight till the enriching
spring unfolds.

But the January tree
all lost and forlorn
is the poorest and coldest
tree of them all.

Preparation

Ask the children to go out looking for interesting trees, leaves, seeds and fruit during the weekend prior to the 'Beech Tree' week and to bring them to school.

Experiencing the poem

1. Read the poem to them, trying to convey its rhythm subtly. Don't over-emphasise the rhymes, but try to make them sound like a kind of echoing effect throughout the poem.
2. Group the children and ask them to read the poem quietly to each other with one reading the first two lines of each verse and the other the second two and so on, and both joining in the chorus. This should establish the echoing effects of the rhymes. Divide the class in half and repeat this, asking the children to speak the words quietly. Try various combinations of their voices.
3. Point out to the children that the poet is imagining that the tree has human attitudes by calling it 'forlorn', 'spendthrift', 'bankrupt' and 'pauper'. List these words and their meanings on the board and add these words: 'encased', 'gems', 'mould', 'beholds', 'fretted' and 'enriching'. Divide the class into groups and ask the groups to discuss the following:
   a) What are the poet's feelings for the beech tree? Write a few lines which show this.
   b) What are the 'coins' and the 'encased gems' really?
   c) What four things does the poet compare the tree to and why?
4. Hold a short plenary session for the groups to present what they decided.

Writing poems about autumn trees, leaves and seeds/nuts

1. Ask the children to think about their own experiences of autumn trees, leaves and seeds/nuts. What did their trees look like? What did they remind them of? How did the leaves feel, sound, look and 'smell? Try to get them to recollect a specific experience rather than general experiences.
2. If it is possible, take the children out to see some trees together so that they can share a real, first hand experience.
3. Tell the children that, for their own autumn poems, they do not have to write rhyming verses, but can write in any form they like so long as it is not a sort of diary entry.
4. If time allows, ask the children to look closely at the leaves they brought and to write haiku about them.
5. Add the poems about trees, leaves and seeds/nuts to the class book of autumn poems and share work.

Week Three Focus: 'Autumn shone forth'[16]

> Autumn shone forth . . . Then grew dark.
> But the world still has life-giving colour:
> In the wither'd flower's dry eye
> A new seed gleams like a spark.
> So small . . . But the spring will come,
> And this seed will be strong enough
> To light up this dull
> and empty place with its light.

Preparation

Ask the children to collect interesting seed-cases from plants, trees, shrubs and wild flowers during the weekend prior to the final week of the project.

Experiencing the poem

1. Tell the children that the writer of the poem, Aleksay Vorobyov, was a poet from an ancient people in Russia, known as the Chuvash, who have their own language and poetry and live about 500 miles east of Moscow.
2. Read the poem, attempting to convey the contrast between autumn shining and then going dark, a theme which is constant throughout.
3. Divide the children into small groups and ask them to practise saying the poem in ways which bring out the contrast between light and dark.
4. Allow each group to perform the poem to the class then ask the groups to discuss the following:
   a) Which things shine in autumn and which things are dull and dark?
   b) What is the poet saying about the seed and what does he mean by 'wither'd flower's dry eye'?

c) What are the poet's feelings about autumn?
5. Hold a plenary session to share these ideas.

Writing poems about the contrasts of autumn and seeds

1. Ask the children to think about any autumn contrasts they have experienced recently. Ask them to try to see or re-experience this in their mind's eye.
2. When they have it in real focus ask them to try to make it into a poem, to 'turn it into words'. Suggest that, perhaps, they will begin with some bold statement then develop examples, but to avoid writing it like a shopping list.
3. If you can, try to make good quality hand lenses and binocular microscopes available for looking closely at the 'withered flowers' and their seeds. Remind the children that Vorobyov described the flower as a 'dry eye' and that this is a *metaphor*. Suggest that in their observations of their plants and flowers and seedcases they might look for their own metaphors and write them as notes while they examine the specimens.
4. Ask the children to use these metaphor notes as a basis for writing poems about their finds.
5. Add the poems about leaves to the class book of autumn poems and share work.

Project 3: Considering natural objects

Purpose: To develop poetry-writing
Length: Six weeks or half a term

Focus i: A collection of natural objects
Focus ii: 'The sheep's skull'

> Corroded by age.
> No longer will it roam
> in green pastures.
> It won't eat the juicy grass.
> The brain chamber
> no longer works.
> Old age was its enemy.
> Holes with hidden secrets in. (Philip, age 12)

Focus iii: 'The Silver Trail'
> The slow animal slimes along.
> The trail of a slippery silver he leaves
> to tell everyone where he treads.
>
> The heavy load on his back
> rocks as if to fall, but the silvery
> animal hangs on to his moving home.

Across the garden he slimes
to his lonely place, to his
quiet corner of this great forest.
(Rebecca, age 11)

Preparation

1. Be on the look-out for interesting natural objects to show the children.
2. Display the poems with the objects. Display these things well and tell your children where you got them, why you like them and what you think they resemble.
3. When they accept the idea that natural objects are suitable for poetry-writing ask the children also to be on the look-out. Encourage them to think that poems are *present* in these objects and it depends on their imaginations to release them, like creatures trapped inside.

Stage One: Whole class writing I

1. Start the poetry-writing session when the children have looked at the objects and read the poems (above).
2. Choose one very significant object such as a log or large skull and show it to the children.
3. Develop the lesson along the following lines:
   a) Make up a name for this object that fits what it looks like. Write it.
   b) Imagine where it might have come from. Vividly describe that place.
   c) Does it remind you of anything else? Imagine hard. Let's see if you can see something else, something different in it. Can you write that vividly?
   d) Read what you have written. Add other names about the place and the something it is like.
4. With younger children conduct the exercise orally, with scribes writing their ideas for them in a notebook rather than the blackboard. Be satisfied with one name or idea from each child.
5. Give the children the opportunity to share ideas as a class or in groups. Ask them to comment and say they have started writing poems. Say that writing a poem is different from writing in their other books, that their imaginations need to be even more switched on.

Stage Two: Whole class writing II

1. Select and arrange the children's ideas so that common ones are together and organise some progression. Write it in large poster form. Practise reading the piece.
2. Show and read the poem to the class and invite them to find their own ideas in it. Invite comments from them. Tell them they have produced a poem for display in the classroom.
3. Repeat Lesson One with a different object. You might find that you need to do this kind of exercise a number of times more with the whole class before moving on to

the making of individual poems. Be patient! You might discover enough in this work for quite some time.

Stage Three: Individual writing I

1. This stage may need several lessons to complete, depending on the time available and the age of the children. The first thing is for each child to find an interesting natural object.
2. When they have all got an object they like, develop the lesson along the following lines:
   a) Look at your object, feel it, smell it, even put your ear close up to it.
   b) Think about it and let your imagination loose. Your imagination is like some spirit that can see objects as if they are inside another world. For instance, once when I looked at the sky my imagination saw a floating castle, a knight on horseback and a large seashore. Try to see your object in that sort of a way.
   c) So look at it and feel it and let your imagination see it differently. When you can do this, make what you see become your poem.
3. Avoid dictionaries, thesauruses and any kind of attention to spelling, punctuation or grammar at this stage. You want the children to respond to the object poetically. This approach is intended to move the children away from factual, descriptive kinds of writing.
4. Have scribes available for younger children or those who lack confidence in writing.
5. When they have finished, ask them to read it through, with questions like these:
   a) Does it say what I want it to say or are there some boring or weak parts to it?
   b) Is it arranged on the page as if it is a poem or does it look like my diary?
   c) Are there any spelling mistakes?
   d) Are there any full stops, capital letters and other punctuation mistakes?
   These questions will then lead to redrafting and, hopefully, to a good final form.
6. There are dangers in this process. It can become a slavishly followed drill, applied to every single piece of work. The children should not be forced to make a fully redrafted poem out of every written response. It is better to develop the idea of a poetry notebook into which many responses are written and only some fully developed.

Stage Four: Individual writing II

1. Arrange the children into small groups to share their poems with one another. The idea here is for each child to read her/his poem and to talk about it. Encourage the children to ask one another questions. The session would be enhanced if the objects were available during the discussions.
2. Bring the children together and invite them to read their poems out to the whole class. Allow this session to develop informally. If a child is reluctant, read the poem yourself.
3. Writing in this way about natural objects should then continue on a regular basis, including trips into the grounds or into the locality outside the school.

Stage Five: Reading and responding

1. Feature the poems in your display and any other suitable ones you or the children find.
2. Ask the children in small groups to select from these and from poems you have found yourself. Ask them to read their selection quietly together and work out meanings. Tell them to talk about their own experiences of these things. Allow use of dictionaries.
3. Ask them also to decide which features make them poems rather than descriptions.

Stage Six: Plenary

1. Organise a plenary session in which the groups present their responses to the poems. Give them time to rehearse this and to work out good, clear readings of the poems.
2. When they have presented their responses, summarise yourself. With groups of older children emphasise the points made about the main features of poems. Stress the use of similes and metaphors in the poems.
3. Arrange presentation of work for the school community, involving the children as follows:
   a) Print one poem per child (essential) and collate into a magazine format with an introduction.
   b) Display handwritten poems with drawings, photographs and paintings.
   c) Read and present discussions of poems. Chorally-speak poems and enact ideas.

References

1. Heaney, S. (1991) *Seeing Things*, Faber, London.
2. Wordsworth, W. 'Ode: Intimations of Immortality from Recollections of Early Childhood' in (1936) *The Poetical works of Wordsworth*, Oxford University Press, London.
3. Theodore Roszak (1972) *Where the Wasteland Ends*, Faber, London.
4. Seamus Heaney 'John Clare's Prog' (1995) *The Redress of Poetry*, Faber, London.
5. Ekwall, E. (1970) *The Concise Oxford Dictionary of English Place-Names*, OUP, Oxford.
6. DfEE (1995) *English in the National Curriculum*, HMSO, London.
7. Hopkins, G.M. 'God's Grandeur' in (1953) Gardner, W.H. (Ed.) *Gerard Manley Hopkins: A Selection of his Poems and Prose*, Penguin, Harmondsworth.
8. Paul Cézanne (1839-1906), French Impressionist painter.
9. Leonardo da Vinci (1452-1519), Italian artist and man of science.
10. Sitwell, E. 'The trees were hissing like green geese' in (1957) *Collected Poems*, Macmillan, London.
11. Hopkins, G.M. 'Spring' in (1953) Gardiner, W. H. (Ed.) *Gerard Manley Hopkins: A Selection of his Poems and Prose*, Penguin, Harmondsworth.
12. Gross, P. 'Snails' in (1984) *The Ice Factory*, Faber, London.
13. Johennese, F. 'the african pot' in Chapman, M. and Dangor, A. (1982) *Voices from Within*, A.D.Donker, Cape.
14. These four haiku appear in (1958) *The Four Seasons*, Peter Pauper Press, New York.
15. Carter, D. 'Beech Tree' in (1998) *Sleeplessness Jungle*, CPP, Mold.
16. Vorobyov, A. 'Autumn Shone Forth' in Aygi, G. (1991) *An Anthology of Chuvash Poetry*, Forest Books, London.

Appendices

Appendix I: Secondary texts for literacy hour lessons

Reception

'The key to the kingdom' (Anonymous)
> This is the key to the kingdom:
> In that kingdom there is a city.
> In that city there is a town.
> In that town there is a street.
> In that street there is a lane.
> In that lane there is a yard.
> In that yard there is a house.
> In that house there is a room.
> In that room there is a bed.
> On that bed there is a basket.
> In that basket there are some flowers.
> Flowers in the basket.
> Basket on the bed.
> Bed in the room.
> Room in the house.
> House in the yard.
> Yard in the lane.
> Lane in the street.
> Street in the town.
> Town in the city.
> City in the kingdom.
> Of that kingdom this is the key.

'Blessings' (Dennis Carter)
> Bless the blue sky,
> bright as a bride.
> Bless the clear sea
> and creatures that hide.
>
> Bless the deep sleep,
> sweet with a dream.
> Bless every flower
> and the fresh stream.

Bless the sun's glow
and the plant's green.
Bless the proud earth,
the eagle's scream.

Bless the Scot's thistle
and the slithery snake.
Bless the smooth fish
that swims in the lake.

Bless every spring,
leaf, stalk and frond.
Bless the spotted egg,
splashes in a pond.

Bless the stray dog,
the tramp in the road.
Bless twice the poor
with their heavy load.

'Up here' (Dennis Carter)

Up here
you can see
far away.

Up here
you can hear
break of day.

Up here
you can feel
thunder play.

Up here
you can smell
fresh cut hay.

Up here
you can taste
the month of May.

Year One

'What's in there?' (Anonymous)
>What's in there?
>Gold and money.
>Where's my share?
>The mousie's run away with it.
>Where's the mousie?
>In her housie.
>Where's her housie?
>In the wood.
>Where's the wood?
>The fire burnt it.
>Where's the fire?
>The water quenched it.
>Where's the water?
>The brown bull drank it.
>Where's the brown bull?
>Behind Burnie's Hill.
>Where's Burnie's Hill?
>All dressed in snow.
>Where's the snow?
>The sun melted it.
>Where's the sun?
>High, high up in the air.

'There I saw' (Anonymous)
>I went up the high hill.
>There I saw a climbing goat.
>I went down by the running rill.
>There I saw a ragged sheep.
>I went out by the roaring sea.
>There I saw a tossing boat.
>I went under the green tree.
>There I saw two doves asleep.

'Ed's head' (Dennis Carter)
>He said,
>"I am Ed."
>Mother said,
>"Go to bed."
>And Mr said,
>"In Ed's head
>are one bird,
>two words,
>three trees,
>four seas,

five dogs,
six logs,
seven goats,
eight ghosts,
nine streams,
ten dreams
in Ed's head
when he's in bed."

Year Two

'The tide rises, the tide falls' (Henry Wadsworth Longfellow)
    The tide rises, the tide falls.
    The twilight darkens, the curlew calls;
    Along the sea-sands damp and brown
    The traveller hastens to the town,
    And the tide rises, the tide falls.

    Darkness settles on roofs and walls,
    But the sea, the sea in the darkness calls;
    The little waves with soft, white hands,
    Efface the footprints in the sands,
    And the tide rises, the tide falls.

    The morning breaks; the steeds in their stalls
    Stamp and neigh, as the hostler calls;
    The day returns, but nevermore
    Returns the traveller to the shore,
    And the tide rises, the tide falls.

'Wild Iron' (Allen Curnow)
    Sea go dark, go dark with wind,
    Feet go heavy, heavy with sand,
    Thoughts go wild, wild with the sound
    Of iron on the old shed swinging, clanging:
    Go dark, go heavy, go wild, go round.
    Dark with the wind,
    Heavy with the sand,
    Wild with the iron that tears at the nail,
    And the foundering shriek of the gale.

'Until I saw the sea' (Lilian Moore)
    Until I saw the sea
    I did not know
    that wind
    could wrinkle water so.

I never knew
that sun
could splinter a whole sea of blue.

Nor
did I know before,
a sea breathes in and out
upon a shore.

Year Three

'The Pelican Chorus' (Extract) (Edward Lear)
>   King and queen of the Pelicans we;
>   No other birds so grand we see!
>   None but we have feet like fins!
>   With lovely, leathery throats and chins!
>   Ploffskin, Pluffskin, Pelican jee!
>   We think no birds so happy as we!
>   Ploffskin, Pluffskin, Pelican jill!
>   We think so then and we thought so still!
>
>   We live on the Nile. The Nile we love.
>   By night we sleep on the cliffs above
>   By day we fish, and at eve we stand
>   On long bare islands of yellow sand.
>   And when the sun sinks slowly down
>   And the great rock walls grow dark and brown,
>   Where the purple river rolls fast and dim
>   And the Ivory Ibis starlike skim,
>   Wing to wing we dance around, –
>   Stamping our feet with a flumpy sound, –
>   Opening our mouths as Pelicans ought,
>   And this is the song we nightly snort; –
>   Ploffskin, Pluffskin, Pelican jee!
>   We think no birds so happy as we!
>   Ploffskin, Pluffskin, Pelican jill!
>   We think so then and we thought so still!

'The Owl' (Lord Tennyson)
>   When cats run home and light is come,
>   And dew is cold upon the ground,
>   And the far-off stream is dumb,
>   And the whirring sail goes round,
>   And the whirring sail goes round;
>   Alone and warming his five wits,
>   The white owl in the belfry sits.

When merry milkmaids click the latch,
And rarely smells the new-mown hay,
And the clock hath sung beneath the thatch
Twice or thrice his roundelay,
Twice or thrice his roundelay;
Alone and warming his five wits,
The white owl in the belfry sits.

'Ducks' Ditty' (Kenneth Graham)
All along the backwater,
Through the rushes tall,
Ducks are a-dabbling
Up tails all!

Ducks' tails, drake's tails,
Yellow feet a-quiver,
Yellow bills all out of sight
Busy in the river!

Slushy green undergrowth
Where the roach swim –
Here we keep our larder,
Cool and full and dim.

Every one for what he likes!
We like to be
Heads down, tails up,
Dabbling free!

High in the blue above
Swifts whirl and call –
We are down a-dabbling
Up tails all!

Year Four

'Meg Merrilies' (John Keats)
Old Meg she was a gipsy,
And lived upon the moors;
Her bed it was the brown heath turf,
And her house was out of doors.
Her apples were swart blackberries,
Her currants, pods o' broom;
Her wine was dew of the wild white rose,
Her book a churchyard tomb.

Her brothers were the craggy hills,
Her sisters larchen trees;
Alone with her great family
She lived as she did please.
No breakfast had she many a morn,
No dinner many a noon,
And 'stead of supper, she would stare
Full hard against the moon.

But every morn, of woodbine fresh
She made her garlanding;
And, every night, the dark glen yew
She wove, and she would sing.
And with her fingers, old and brown,
She plaited mats of rushes,
And gave them to the cottagers
She met among the bushes.

Old Meg was brave as Margaret Queen,
And tall as Amazon:
An old red blanket cloak she wore,
A chip-hat had she on.
God rest her aged bones somewhere –
She died full long agone.

'Old Man' (Dennis Carter)
On this cold
and bitter day
the chatty little
old man hurries
head down from
the corner shop.

Thickly and quickly
his breath pours
out like smoke.
His eyes are sparks
as he stares
straight ahead
on this cold
and bitter day.

Grimly and thinly
his tight lips
put out his words.

He does not say
hello but scuttles
quickly home.

The chatty little
old man thinks
of warmth for
in his arms he holds
a new bag of coal
on this cold
and oh! so bitter
this cold and
bitter day.

'The Ugly Child' (Elizabeth Jennings)
I heard them say I'm ugly.
I hoped it wasn't true.
I looked into the mirror
To get a better view,
And certainly my face seemed
Uninteresting and sad.
I *wish* that either it was good
Or else just very bad.

My eyes are green, my hair is straight,
My ears stick out, my nose
Has freckles on it all the year,
I'm skinny as a hose.
If only I could look as I
Imagine I might be.
Oh, all the crowds would turn and bow.
They don't – because I'm me.

Appendix II: A list of other valuable poems

It is rather artificial to divide up poetry according to different ages as most good quality poems are suitable for any age. The poems listed here have been successfully used with the age group suggested, but please bear in mind that many of them are suitable for the other age groups. The lists are also intended to supplement the poems which teachers have already accumulated. They represent a small group of well-tested poems.

Key Stage 1

These poems for infants are offered as a supplement to the range of nursery rhymes, finger rhymes and other traditional verses available in any good nursery rhyme book.

'The Midnight Mouse', Christian Morgenstern, in *The Gallows Songs*, University of California Press.

'The Midnight Forest', Judith Nicholls, in *The Midnight Forest*, Faber.

'The Moon and the Stars', William Carlos Williams, in *Collected Poems*, Carcanet.

'Omen', Birago Diop, in *Flock of Words*, Bodley Head.

'The Hare in the Moon', Judith Wright, in *Selected Poems*, Carcanet.

'Christabel' (extract), Samuel Taylor Coleridge, in *Poems*, Dent Dutton.

'Night', Georgi Djagarov, in *Poets of Bulgaria*, Forest Books.

'The Sea Shell', Marin Sorescu, in *Selected Poems*, Bloodaxe.

'The Intruder' and 'The Snail', James Reeves, in *The Wandering Moon and Other Poems*, Penguin.

'Fog', Carl Sandburg, in *Complete Poems*, Holt Reinhardt and Winston.

'The Duck' and 'The Cow', Ogden Nash, in *Candy is Dandy*, Mandarin.

'The Quangle Wangle's Hat', Edward Lear, in *A Book of Bosh*, Penguin.

'hist whist' and 'little tree', e.e.cummings, in *Selected Poems*, Faber.

'I Am Boj' and 'Elephant Poems', Adrian Mitchell, in *Nothingmas Day*, Allison & Busby.

'I like to stay up', 'Granny, Granny Please Comb My Hair', 'Have You Ever Seen', Grace Nicholls, in *I Like that Stuff*, Cambridge.

'Leaves in the Yard', Hal Summers, in *Tomorrow is My Love*, Oxford.

'The Pobble who has no Toes' and 'The Jumblies', Edward Lear, in *A Book of Bosh*, Penguin.

'maggie, milly, molly and may', e.e.cummings, in *Selected Poems*, Faber.

'Shadows', Patricia Hubbell, in *Catch Me a Wind*, Atheneum.

Key Stage 2: Years 3 and 4

'The Sleeping Beauty', Edith Sitwell, in *Collected Poems*, Macmillan.

'The Workings of the Wind', James Berry, in *I Like that Stuff*, CUP.

'Running Lightly Over Spongy Ground', Theodore Roethke, in *Collected Poems*, Faber.

'The Coming of the Cold', Theodore Roethke, in *Collected Poems*, Faber.

'Cat in the Weather', May Swenson, in *To Mix with Time*, Charles Scribner.

'This smoky winter morning', Charles Reznikoff, in *Junior Voices - 3*, Penguin.

'Thunder and Lightning', James Kirkup, in *Junior Voices - 3*, Penguin.

'Cloud Mobile', May Swenson, in *To Mix with Time*, Charles Scribner.

'Tree at my Window', Robert Frost, in *Selected Poems*, Penguin.
'Above the Dock' and 'Autumn', T. E. Hulme in *The Faber Book of Modern Poetry*, Faber.
'Song's Eternity', John Clare, in *Selected Poems*, Dent Dutton.
'The Akond of Swat', Edward Lear, in *The Faber Book of Nonsense Verse*, Faber.
'John Barleycorn', Robert Burns, in *Poems*, Dent Dutton.
'The Jabberwocky', Lewis Carroll, in *Alice Through the Looking-glass*, Cassell.
'Pied Beauty', G. M. Hopkins, in *Selected Poems*, Penguin.
'Stufferation' and 'Nothingmas Day', Adrian Mitchell, in *Nothingmas Day*, Allison & Busby.

Key Stage 2: Years 5 and 6

'In the Beginning', Phoebe Hesketh, in *Netting the Sun*, Enitharmon.
'Recollection', Shimmer Chinodya, in *Voices from Within*, A. D. Donker.
'Cats no less liquid', A.S.J. Tessimond, in *Not Love Perhaps*, Autolycus.
'The Cataract of Lodore', Robert Southey, in *Poems*, Dent Dutton.
'The Ruined City', Pao Chao, in *Poems of Solitude*, UNESCO.
'The Collier', Vernon Watkins, in *Ballad of the Mari Llwyd*, Faber.
'Y Diwaith', T.Rowland Hughes, in *Poetry of Wales 1930-1970*, Gomer.
'The Birth of Moshesh', D.G.T.Bereng, in *Voices from Within*, A.D.Donker.
'Rhiannon', D.Gwenallt Jones, in *Poetry of Wales 1930-1970*, Gomer.
'Lleu', Brian Martin Davies, in *Poetry of Wales 1930-1970*, Gomer.
'God's Grandeur' and 'Spring', G.M.Hopkins, in *Selected Poems*, Penguin.
'Spring Nature Notes', Ted Hughes, in *Season Songs*, Faber.
'La Belle Dame Sans Merci', John Keats, *Poems*, Dent Dutton.
'Roman Wall Blues', W.H.Auden, in *Collected Shorter Poems*, Faber.
'Full Fathom Five', 'Where the bee sucks', and 'Come unto these yellow sands' in William Shakespeare, *The Tempest*, Routledge.
'The old deep sing-song', Carl Sandburg, in *Complete Poems*, Holt Reinhardt and Winston.
'Spell of Creation', Kathleen Raine, in *Collected Poems*, Hamish Hamilton.
'Spring is like a perhaps hand', e.e.cummings, in *Selected Poems*, Faber.
'Weathers' and 'The Darkling Thrush', Thomas Hardy, in *The Complete Poems*, Macmillan.
'Dewdrop', Ted Walker, in *The Night Bathers*, Cape.
'Blackberry-Picking' and 'Trout', Seamus Heaney, in *Death of a Naturalist*, Faber
'The Meadow Mouse', Theodore Roethke, in *Collected Poems*, Faber.
'Thistles', Jon Stallworthy, in *Root and Branch*, Chatto and Windus.
'Poppies in July', Sylvia Plath, in *Ariel*, Faber.
'Flowers', Jean Rimbaud, in *A Flock of Words*, Bodley Head.
'Starry Snail', Vasko Popa, in *Selected Poems*, Penguin.
'The Locust', Anonymous Madagascan poem, in *A Flock of Words*, Bodley Head.
'Worm', Jeremy Reed, in *Nero*, Cape.
'Macavity, the Mystery Cat', T.S.Eliot, in *Old Possum's Book of Practical Cats*, Faber.
'My Brother Bert', Ted Hughes, in *Meet My Folks*, Faber.

Appendix III: A list of useful anthologies

Benson, G. *This poem doesn't rhyme*, Penguin.
Berry, J., Nicholls, G., Nicholls, J., Scannell, V. and Sweeney, M. *We Couldn't Provide Fish Thumbs*, Macmillan.
Craft, R. *The song that sings the bird*, Young Lion.
Davies, N. and Rae, S. *Welcome to the Party*. B.B.C.
Fisher, R. *Minibeasts*, Faber.
Fisher, R. *Pet Poems*, Faber.
Godden, R. *Cockcrow to Starlight*, Macmillan.
Graham, E. *A Puffin Book of Verse*, Puffin.
Grigson, G. *The Faber Book of Nonsense Verse*, Faber.
Harrison, M. and Stuart-Clark, C. *The New Dragon Book of Verse*, Oxford.
Harrison, M. and Stuart-Clark, C. *The Oxford Book of Christmas Poems*, Oxford.
Harvey, A. *He said, she said, they said*, Blackie.
Harvey, A. *Of Caterpillars, Cats and Cattle*, Penguin.
Heaney, S. and Hughes, T. *The Rattle Bag*, Faber.*
Lewis, M. *Messages*, Faber.
Mackay, D. *A Flock of Words*, Bodley Head.*
Mitchell, A. *The Orchard Book of Poems*, Orchard Books.*
Mosley, I. *The Green Book of Poetry*, Frontier.
Nicholls, G. *Can I buy a slice of sky?* Hodder.*
Opie, I. and Opie, P. *The Puffin Book of Nursery Rhymes*, Penguin.
Philip, N. *The New Oxford Book of Children's Verse*, Oxford.
Quinn, B. and Cashman, S. *The Wolfhound Book of Irish Poems for young people*, Wolfhound.
Rosen, M. *A World of Poetry*, Kingfisher.*
Smith, J.A. *The Faber Book of Children's Verse*, Faber.
Styles, M., *I like that stuff*, Cambridge.*
Summerfield, G. *Junior Voices, 1, 2, 3 and 4*, Penguin.*
Webb, K. (Ed.) *I Like This Poem*, Puffin.

*A particularly good source of multicultural poems.

Good collections of haikus:
Basho, *On Love and Barley*, Penguin.
Akmakjian, H. *Snow Falling from a Bamboo Leaf*, Capra.
Stryk, L. and Ikemoto, T. *The Penguin Book of Zen Poetry*, Penguin.

For a copy of Carter, D. *Sleeplessness Jungle*, Clwyd Poetry Project, Mold (ISBN 0 9533499 0 X) send a cheque for £5.45 (incl. 50p. p&p) to the author at Pentre Farm, Woodhill, Oswestry, Shropshire SY10 9AS. Tel: 01691 656320.

Index